Hindu Culture

An Introduction

THE *Hindu Culture* SERIES

Hindu Culture

An Introduction

Transcribed from Lectures

By

SWAMI TEJOMAYANANDA

CENTRAL CHINMAYA MISSION TRUST
MUMBAI - 400 072.

Chinmaya Publications
Main Office
P.O. Box 129,
Piercy, CA 95587, USA

Chinmaya Mission West Publication Division
Distribution Office
560 Bridgetown Pike
Langhorne, Pennysylvania 19053, USA
Tel. : (215) 396 0390 Fax : (215) 396 9710
www.chinmaya publications.org

Central Chinmaya Mission Trust
Sandeepany Sadhanalaya
Saki Vihar Road, Mumbai 400 072. India.
Tel.:091-22-8572367,8575806
Fax : 091-22-8573065
Email : chinmaya@bom2.vsnl.net.in

Printed in India in 1994 - 1000 copies
Reprinted in India in Dec. 1996- 2000 copies
Reprinted in India in June 1999- 1000 copies
Reprinted in India in June 2000-2000 copies

Prashant Art Printers
Unit 105, Ruby Industrial Estate,
Chincholi Bunder Road, Off. Link Road,
Malad (W), Mumbai - 400 064. India.
Tel. : 091-22-8762767, 8767444

Credits :
Cover concept by Peter Trucker
Cover design by Fabian West
Colour photograph on the cover by Helem Desai.
Library of Congress Catalog Number 93-70108
ISBN N - 1-880687-05-4

Contents

PART TWO

THE LANGUAGE OF SYMBOLISM

PART THREE

THE ESSENCE OF DHARMA

PART FOUR

THE EPICS

Preface

The Hindu culture is founded upon the sacred scriptures of the Vedas, which provided the enduring foundations upon which this most ancient of civilizations was built. These sacred scriptures are revered even today, for they contain revelations of eternal Truth and embody the spiritual and cultural heritage of the Hindu people.

The term "Hindu" was coined by the Persians to designate a group of people living east of the river Sindhu or Indus. These people referred to their religion as *sanātana dharma* (eternal *dharma*)—eternal—because the principles it proclaimed were of a universal nature. Their thinkers (the rishis), being subjective scientists, had experienced and touched a deep cord within, far beyond the physical, mental, and intellectual layers, which allowed them to see all life as interconnected. They saw the One manifested throughout the universe so that everything was sacred to them. When life itself is honored and belief in the holiness of all life is fostered, one cannot help but acquire a deep sense of reverence for life. The Hindu culture evolved out of this expanded vision.

Civilization flourishes with the promotion of culture, but when the cultural values deteriorate, civilization declines. This can be seen, for instance, with the fall of the Greek and Roman empires. When higher ideals are no longer pursued and fundamental principles of civilization are ignored, the result will be great moral confusion. This is the unfortunate condition of the world today.

The great religious masters of India have time and again revived their glorious culture. In no other philosophical system in the world have these values been so beautifully and exhaustively dealt with as in the sacred books of India. These cherished books offer nourishing inspiration and guidance. The great spiritual authors speak to us of visions and values that reflect their realization of the One in the many.

Hindu Culture evolved out of a series of lectures given by Swami Tejomayananda in Los Altos in 1991. The lectures were originally designed to instruct those individuals who were teaching children and youth. Thus Swamiji brings out all the vital aspects and dynamism of this culture. That we can still hear the echo of his words reverberating in our hearts long after we have heard or read them, shows the incredible power of his communication skills. By explaining the value of a value, he motivates us to incorporate time-honored principles into our lives. When we realize that our actions influence the entire society, the value system that we live by and the choices that we make become of paramount importance.

In Part One, Swami Tejomayananda examines the two basic types of culture, material and spiritual, and emphasizes the need for culture. He then shows how the various texts of the Hindu cultural tradition all use different ways and means to inculcate value systems.

Part Two explores the art of symbolism. God-symbolism has a language of its own, and we need the help of a Vedantic master to grasp this subtle science. Understanding the deep inner meaning represented by the symbols is to discover at the same time profound philosophical truths.

Swami Tejomayananda explains the full significance of *sanātana dharma* in Part Three. He points out that adherence to values lends a sense of dignity, direction, and purpose to every individual.

In Part Four we are encouraged to enrich our lives by studying the immortal epics, the *Rāmāyana* and the *Mahābhārata*. We see the entire gamut of human emotions displayed throughout these epics, and marvel at the beauty of a culture that can impart ethical and spiritual training in such a natural way.

A culture based on a dynamic and practical philosophy which indicates the goal of life and the many ways to reach it cannot help but have an enduring quality about it. These fundamental ideas have provided a spiritual base and direction to the Hindu culture throughout the ages. Scriptures assure us that there will be true guides of the spirit in every age leading humankind to its ultimate fulfillment. Swami Tejomayananda is such a guide. By giving an overview of this great culture he helps us reassess our value systems and motivates us to live these universal principles.

M.L.

PART ONE

Introduction to the Vedas

Man's control of nature external
is called civilization.
His control of nature internal
is called culture.

Swami Chinmayananda

Just as physics, biology, and other sciences are not the exclusive property of any one country, or of people in a particular era or age, but are universally applicable, irrespective of time and age; similarly the science of living, as pronounced by the rishis in Vedanta, visualizes a plan of life to suit all people, at all times, everywhere.

Swami Chinmayananda

Everyone of us may not be able at once to achieve the infinite expansion of universal oneness, but all of us are trying. Religion's original task was to help us in gradually achieving this elevated vision. To lift the limited and selfish human being from his passion, greed, and hatred to this loftier vision of the world was the essential ideal of religion.

Swami Chinmayananda

I

The Definition of Culture

The word "culture" is very well known to all of us. But when it comes to defining this word, we find that it is not very easy. Swami Chinmayananda has explained that when a group of people live together for a long time in a particular geographical area, living certain values, the special individuality or fragrance that emanates from that group is said to be their culture.

In this definition of culture the four important factors are: that a group of people must exist, that they must live together in a particular area, that they must live there for a long period of time, and that they respect certain common values of life. Only in such a situation will the unique characteristics of those people be created. If the individuals are spread out—one living here, another one there—or if they are constantly roaming about with no values in common, then you will not find any recognizable culture emerging from them.

This special mark or characteristic that develops under the above circumstances is called culture, which is not the characteristic of only one individual, but of the group as a whole.

There is a difference between the community's and the individual's nature, which I would like to explain.

When a certain individual behaves in a particular way, we generally say, "That is his nature." But when a community responds to different situations in a particular way, we say it is its culture. The difference is that with respect to one person's mode of behavior, we call it nature; and with respect to a community, we call it culture. They influence each other, no doubt, for the individual will influence the total and the total also affects the behavior of the individual. But let us first understand the meaning and significance of each term by itself.

In Sanskrit, we call the individual's nature *saṃskāra*. In a family with three or four children, though each is born into the same culture, we find that each individual behaves differently. Then we ask: If they are all born in the same family, the same culture, and in the same country, then why does each person behave differently? We answer that it is his nature (*saṃskāra*, *svabhāva*); and his actions are in accordance with those particular tendencies. When it comes to a group, however, we say that the group's mode of behavior and response is its culture.

Cultures differ very much from place to place. Even in the Eastern hemisphere, for instance, the Middle Eastern countries are different from the Far Eastern countries, and India is again different from both. When we come to the Western countries, we also find that the European culture is different from the American culture; thus even though we may say "Western culture," many differences are contained within this generalization. Having said this much, we will now look at the actual Sanskrit word for culture, and see its meaning and deeper implication.

Prakṛti and Vikṛti

In Sanskrit, the word for culture is *saṃskṛti*. *Kṛtam* means "that which is done," *sam* means "very well"; *saṃskṛti* means "that which is very well made, very well refined." Therefore, even the Sanskrit language itself is that which is a well-refined, purified language.

In terms of behavior, when we speak of culture we also mean a kind of refinement. We often say that an individual is "cultured," his behavior is "cultured," although he may not necessarily be an educated person. Many times, in fact, an educated man may be a brute because being truly cultured is different from merely being formally educated. But to fully understand this concept of *saṃskṛti*, we must understand two other basic points.

The first point is the concept of *prakṛti*, which we generally translate as "nature." The inherent nature or tendency of a thing is called its *prakṛti*. For example, animals have urges such as hunger, thirst, feelings of fear or insecurity, and the need for sleep, and they live according to these desires or urges. This is defined as their nature.

A human being also has these same feelings of fear, hunger, thirst, and desire for progeny. These are natural urges. Therefore, when a person feels hunger and goes in search of food, the action is called *prakṛti*—action in accordance with nature. There is nothing wrong in this.

As long as we are acting according to nature, there is no problem. But there is a difference between the urges of an animal and a human being. The animal's urges and pursuits are controlled by nature; they remain within limits and never transgress nature. Therefore, the animal's behavior is true to its *prakṛti*.

For instance, when a dog has satisfied its hunger, it will not eat anymore. In the ashram where I was studying, some three or four dogs would remain around the kitchen and dining hall when the food was being served, and afterwards they would be fed. If there was more food than the dogs could eat at that time, they would each dig a hole in the earth and keep the food there until later. When they became hungry, they would go back, dig up the food, and eat it. Also when dogs are sick, they will not eat food at all, but only different grasses—as medicine. Nature has given them this understanding.

But a human being! Whatever sickness he may have, even if his stomach is upset, the first question he will ask the doctor is, "What can I eat?" He just cannot control his eating. So the difference is that the animals remain true to their *prakṛti*; they do not transgress it. Even the animal's desire for progeny is according to season. Everything is controlled.

In Sanskrit, there is another word, *vikṛti*, which in this context, I will translate as "perversion." When some urge or desire grows out of proportion and we transgress the control and limits of *prakṛti*, it is *vikṛti*, perversion; no longer *prakṛti*.

When I feel tired, naturally I sleep for some time to revive myself and then again begin to work. Here, the sleep is not a problem, it is not a *vikṛti*. But if one sleeps for sixteen hours at a stretch, then something is wrong; it is not natural and is therefore *vikṛti*. There are people who sleep ten to twelve hours and still say, "I think I got up too early this morning!" But twelve hours of sleep is abnormal and unnatural and is called *vikṛti*.

In the same way, when I am hungry and want to eat, this is *prakṛti*. However, if I continue to eat like a glutton, and in order to satisfy my taste buds I am ready to do anything (kill animals, and even destroy nature to fulfill my desire), then this is perversion.

I once heard a story about a Roman emperor who was so terribly fond of eating that he used to overeat and afterwards take medicine in order to vomit. Then he would again begin to eat! Even when we hear about such a thing we feel nauseous! This obsession of the emperor with eating is *vikṛti*.

All living beings have natural urges, and as long as they live within their limits it is not a perversion; it is simple *prakṛti*. In the case of animals, their behavior is controlled by nature itself, but in the case of human beings, there is a difference.

The human being is blessed with the faculty of thinking, which allows a lot of freedom. And what is that freedom? I can either destruct or construct myself; both are possible. Thus this faculty of thinking is a blessing if we use it rightly. If we do not know how to use it properly, it can become a curse. Our *prakṛti*, our nature, can become an obsession, an abnormality. This is why psychology books contain sections on abnormal psychology, dealing with the thought and behavioral patterns of people whose nature has taken the form of perversion.

The Need to Refine our Behavior

What we need to do is to control, discipline, and refine our behavior. In the human being, nature has released its control and said, "Now you are blessed with an intellect. You have the faculty of reason and discrimination; therefore, you can choose and know what is good for you and live accordingly." If a person can live like this, it is good; if not, he becomes even worse than an animal.

In order to refine the person, to prevent *prakṛti* from turning into *vikṛti*, what we need is *saṃskṛti*, or culture. Mere education or rising to higher positions, gaining more money and power, will not necessarily make one a cultured person. One's mind may yet remain animalistic.

Sri Ramakrishna Paramahamsa used to say that our minds are like that of a vulture. A vulture flies very high in the sky, but where are his eyes? They are on the dead body lying on the ground; the moment he sees the dead body he swoops down to eat it! We are also like that. A person may fly to a very "high" position of political, economic, or financial power, and others may even be prostrating to him. But where is his mind? This is, as we say, "corruption in high places." So when our mind is like that of a vulture fixed on low, base things, we need culture in order to fly high, not only materially, but morally and spiritually as well. Then the mind rises to true spiritual heights.

It is difficult to explain what culture is, and it cannot be taught through discourses. As Swamiji (Swami Chinmayananda) says, "Culture cannot be taught, but it can be caught [by the children]." Just as children automatically "pick up" whichever language is spoken at home without being taught, culture is also "picked up" the same way. If we constantly instruct the children on do's and don'ts, yet we ourselves live differently, they will not follow our instructions. Example always speaks louder than words, this is why culture cannot be taught merely by words.

Living life based on noble values is the most important point concerning culture. Why do we need values? Why do we need to respect them and live by them? Because in the human being, there is every danger of his nature transgressing its limits and becoming a perversion. This is what we see in the world today: greed for money, power, and position. No one knows what will happen next. Yet we cannot just blame the political leaders because these tendencies are in our minds as well and we act accordingly. It is just that one who has more power will terrorize more, that is all.

We find this same behavior in some school children also, for some of them are monster-like in creating trouble for others.

Concerning the worst-behaved child in the classroom, a teacher once said, "What is great about him is that his attendance record at school is one hundred percent!" The teacher is thinking to herself, "Stay home at least one day, please!" But no, he attends every day, and every day he creates problems!

There are bullies in the classroom as well as in world politics, and it shows the absence of something—the absence of refinement. One may be rich, a well-educated scholar, or a politically powerful person, but he may not have the refinement of character which we call *saṃskṛti*. The beauty of a person does not lie in his physical, educational, or other capabilities, but in his culture, which expresses itself every moment in his day-to-day life.

Two Kinds of Culture

The third question to be asked is: "How many different kinds of culture are there?"

As I said earlier, there are many communities and nations, and each one has its own culture or tradition. Nevertheless, we mainly divide or classify these cultures into two general groups: spiritual culture, and material or materialistic culture. These words will also have to be understood very carefully.

In Sanskrit, spiritual culture is called *adhyātmic saṃskṛti*, and materialistic culture is known as *bhautic saṃskṛti*.

These terms are often misunderstood, for we generally think that materialistic culture means to go on enjoying—just to eat, drink, and be merry! But this is a very superficial way of looking at it. At the same time, people have the notion that to be spiritual one has to renounce everything, to run off to the Himalayas, and just sit there! So one person is saying, "Enjoy the world," and the other is saying, "Escape! Run away from this world. Everything in it is bad! Go somewhere far away and contemplate."

Others have the notion that spiritual culture is very good, but materialism is very bad—that the people of a particular culture and their country are bad! Each person becomes proud of his own culture. The follower of the materialistic culture who does not fully understand spiritual culture says, "You people are just getting poorer and poorer; your culture is useless." Then those of the spiritual culture say to the materialist, "You are only running after objects, going through stress and strain, tension, and temptation. What kind of a life is that?" So each person thinks his own culture is superior. Most people do not have a clear understanding of what material culture and spiritual culture really mean, for it is not that one is good and the other is bad.

Some teenagers and youngsters say, "Oh, we know what spiritual culture is: When you see an elderly person, you must prostrate to him. That is called spiritual culture—prostration, salutation." And some parents insist on it so much that they push the child's head down to touch the elder's feet, and the child just thinks, "Why should I smell his feet?" Is this what spiritual culture is?

In Sanskrit, the term *bhautic vāda* (materialism) comes from the word *bhūta*, "element"; *bhautic* means "elemental." One generally takes as real only that which is directly in front of one's eyes, which is tangible and in a material form. The philosophical basis of *bhautic vāda* is "seeing is believing." Thus, whatever I see is real. Perception of the material tangible world is given complete validity and reality and something that is not seen, known, or is not verifiable by scientific experiment in the laboratory is not accepted as real. Materialism means faith in matter, the physical things that are perceived by our senses. This is why some people who have studied only a little bit of science say, "What is religion? Religion is only a matter of faith, and you are just accepting what you do not see."

I met a man a few days ago in Washington, D.C., who, while a student in Delhi, had met Dr. Radhakrishnan, the then vice-president of India. He had asked Dr. Radhakrishnan a question: "Sir, since you are a great philosopher, can you explain the difference between science and religion, as there seems to be a contradiction between the two? Religion speaks of something that is not seen and people have faith in that. But in science one says, 'No, I only accept what I see,' so it appears that scientists are anti-religious."

Dr. Radhakrishnan gave a very nice answer. He said, "It is

something like this: A little science takes you away from religion but more of it brings you nearer religion." Dr. Radhakrishnan meant that those students who have studied only a little bit of science—atomic physics, particle physics, and so on—speak of religion and God in derogatory terms. Einstein would not agree with this negative view, as is evident from his writings.

Thus the materialist has faith in, and bases his life upon, the supposed validity and reality of seen things, whereas spiritual philosophy says, "Yes, whatever is seen is fine, but do not think that truth is only that which is seen by the senses." There are many things that exist even though you cannot see them. Sense perception is not the only valid means of knowing what is real. Through the senses we can only observe objects of the world, but there are things that lie beyond sense perception and different means exist for knowing them.

In the next chapter, I will further discuss these two types of culture, their respective values of life, the bases of these values, and the source of knowledge of the fundamental values of the Hindu culture. We will study this step by step in small doses.

II

The Basis of Culture

There are basically two different kinds of culture: the materialistic culture, or *bhautic saṃskṛti*, and the spiritual culture, or *adhyātmic saṃskṛti.* The difference between them lies in the particular philosophy of life that they uphold. From these two standpoints all other varieties of culture arise.

We should understand then that it is not the world itself that is good or bad, but how we look at the world that matters. Depending on our attitude and values our ways of living will be different. Neither philosophy should be taken to an extreme, but each should be kept in balance, for it is only when we go to extremes that the two philosophies seem to contradict each other.

Materialistic Culture

The philosophy of materialistic culture gives the most reality to that which is solid, gross, tangible, and perceivable by the senses. Further investigation into the nature of matter is emphasized, along with the application of that knowledge in practical ways to make our lives more comfortable. The materialist does not accept the existence of the unseen, or if he does feel that something other than the seen exists, he pays only lip service to it and makes no further inquiry into it. Such a person is adventurous. Therefore, he wants to know what is in the depths of the ocean, deep in the earth, in outer space, or on different planets. Such investigation is done through the sense organs, the mind, the intellect, and through various kinds of apparatuses and equipments, just as we see today: microscopes, telescopes, spectroscopes, and so on. All this is to find out what is far, far away, deep down below, or what is extremely subtle, as in the study of molecular physics, atomic physics, and particle physics.

Another aspect of the materialistic philosophy is the idea that this whole world is meant for our enjoyment. The materialist believes that he must conquer nature and make it useful for his own personal life. Naturally there will be material progress in such a culture as a result of this way of thinking, for whenever and in whichever direction a person applies his mind, progress is the certain result. These, then, are the dominant thoughts in the materialistic philosophy.

Spiritual Culture

In the philosophy of spiritual culture, that which is unseen is given greater importance than that which is seen. The existence of matter is not totally denied, but it is said that that which is seen is not alone what is real—there is something, though unseen and invisible, which cannot be said to be nonexistent. In fact, the spiritual person believes that that which is unseen is what controls the visible, perceptible world of objects.

For example, the body moves about and carries on all its functions, but because of what does it function? We are not able to find this out through the sense organs or any other instrument of knowledge. The invisible, then, which appears to have total control over that which is visible, is the subject of inquiry for the person following the spiritual philosophy. Spiritually minded people are also adventurous, but their adventure lies in investigating into the unseen that is not experienced through the senses.

If a human being has a tremendous attachment for seen objects of the world; if he is fascinated, attracted, and finds himself gravitating toward matter, it is not a surprise or to be wondered at because our senses are constantly seeing color and form, experiencing sound, taste, and touch, which are all tempting to the sense organs. But what is more surprising and fascinating to me is that so many people are attracted toward that which is invisible, which many may never have had any glimpse of, yet for which they are ready to give up money, material and political power, and all comforts. People of this type exist in every age. Though truly spiritual people are few in the world, there are many religious people who have not seen God, yet have faith in their concept of Him. Is not this attraction of the human being toward the invisible more surprising and fascinating than his or her attraction toward objects? Humanity has an inherent curiosity in the unseen. We want to know what exists after death, and only days after someone dies we ask, "What happens after death?" That something which exists, though unseen, is called Spirit, and the inquiry into it is the basis of what we call spiritual culture.

Whereas in a materialistic culture the idea exists of conquering and making use of nature for personal convenience, spiritual culture attempts to understand and to live in harmony with nature and finally go beyond it. This is a very different approach than that of the materialistic one. The spiritual philosophy, in the end, totally transforms the life of the individual as well as that of the entire community.

Having touched upon the broad differences between spiritual and materialistic cultures, we will now describe them in greater detail.

The Source of Cultural Values

When any community, society, or nation follows a particular set of values of life, it must be assumed that these values were given or propounded by someone. There is always some basis or source from which these values are taken, expounded, and set forth for the people.

In communist countries, all of whose systems we can now see as breaking down, the governments had earlier denounced everything having to do with God and religion. They said religion was a "bogus" concept, the opiate of the masses, something by which the people would get intoxicated and go mad; so they closed down all the temples and churches. Some time ago, however, the last Soviet president said that "the greatest mistake we made was to throw religion out of our country."

They refused to accept the Bible, the Vedas, or any other scripture. But then what did they do? They followed the philosophy of one man—Karl Marx! What happens is that if we refute one book, we take up another; we denounce one person but then start following another.

Karl Marx said that religion was a dangerous thing. We do not know exactly what he understood by the word "religion" or what was being practiced in the name of religion at that time, so we do not say that he was totally wrong. In his own context, he may have been correct. We could also criticize the misuse of religion, but this does not mean that the whole idea of religion should be thrown out! We should try to find out the true meaning of religion and how to apply it to our lives in the best way possible. In the beginning, the Soviet Union had built up its society on the philosophy called Marxism, but now we see the sad condition of that country. This is because a human being needs more than just food, shelter, and clothing. "Man does not live by bread alone!"

The point is that there is always a foundation or source from which the philosophy of a culture springs forth. The values that are followed by that culture are propounded by someone, whether it be by one person or a group. When we look at countries of Islamic culture, the Middle Eastern and Arab nations, we see that the word of the Prophet (Mohammed) is the source and foundation upon which the whole culture is built. Likewise, in the Christian countries, the Bible is the source of people's values. When there is no deep-rooted set of values or foundation upon which a culture is based, we find that its philosophy keeps changing every five to ten years and that the people follow whichever ideas are more popular at that time. In either case, however, there is always some particular value which predominates, providing the foundation for the direction of the culture at that time.

III

The Vedas and Culture

The culture of a community or nation is based upon the values that its people live and uphold in their lives. These values themselves are derived from a philosophy or "source book" propounded either by one person or by a group of people. For the Hindu culture, the Vedas are the "source book" [of knowledge for its philosophy and values].

The Veda, which was originally one, is now classified into four: the *Ṛg*, *Sāma*, *Yajur*, and *Atharva Vedas*. The word *Veda* is derived from the Sanskrit verbal root *vid*, "to know," and is generally translated as "the treasure of knowledge" or "the source or means of knowledge." Although many people think that the Hindu culture is completely of the "other world" and gives no consideration to this present world, the fact is that the Vedas contain knowledge in every field of worldly science and come under the headings of the *ṣaḍaṅgas* (six limbs): phonetics (*śikṣā*), the code of rituals (*kalpa*), grammar (*vyākaraṇa*), etymology (*nirukta*), literature (*chandas*), and astronomy (*jyotiṣa*).

Along with these six branches, there are also the four *Upavedas*, or sub-Vedas, consisting of the four sciences of medicine (*Āyurveda*), archery (*Dhanurveda*), music (*Gāndharvaveda*), and architecture (*Sthāpatyaveda*). Since the ancient tradition of passing on these branches of knowledge from teacher to student has been lost, we think that the Vedas contain nothing relevant for us today. The fact is that the Vedas consider all aspects of human life.

The Purpose of Life

We shall now touch upon the main topic in the Vedas as far as it concerns the theme of culture.

Most of us will accept the fact that this human life is meant for more than just indulging in pleasures. Though eating, drinking, and enjoying are a part of life, we cannot say that this is all there is to life. The human being is distinguished from other creatures because he possesses an intellect, the faculty of understanding and thinking. The purpose of the intellect is to know the truth or essence of things that are perceived by our senses.

In Sanskrit, two words make this distinction between an animal and a human being very clear. The Sanskrit word for animal is *paśu*, derived etymologically from *paśyati iti paśuḥ*—that which "sees" only externally, which takes things at face value, giving no thought to what the truth of a thing is. For the animal there is no need to look deeper, for an object is generally useful only insofar as it is edible.

The English word "man," however, is derived from the Sanskrit word *manuṣya,* from the root *man,* meaning "to think." *Manuṣya* suggests that for the human being it is not enough to merely see an object physically, but that he should think about and know the truth behind it. The purpose of human life, therefore, is to know the truth, and is not for *bhoga,* or enjoyment, alone.

Knowledge of the Truth gives us real victory in life. And what is this victory? It is the conquering of our own minds, so that we are not perturbed by every little change that takes place in the world around us. This total victory over our minds is won not by compulsion nor by artificially induced methods that suspend the mind temporarily, but by knowledge and understanding alone.

The Spiritual Significance of Navaratri

Let us first discuss the values of the Indian culture and the subject matter of the Vedas in terms of the Navaratri festival.

Even though Hindus celebrate this festival every year, most

have no idea of the significance of Navaratri. Last year, an American boy who was attending my talks regularly had gone to see a Navaratri festival in a Gujarati community where they were doing the *garba* dance throughout the night. He asked some of his Hindu friends what it meant, but they were unable to explain.

What colossal ignorance! Here a Westerner wants to know the meaning of Navaratri and no one can tell him. They could only say, "Oh, it is a nice thing, isn't it? A social gathering. Just enjoy, sing and dance, eat, and then go!" We should know, however, the meaning of this important religious festival, which I will explain briefly.

Rātri means "night" and *nava* means "nine." At Navaratri ("nine nights"), the Goddess is worshiped in Her various forms as Durga, Lakshmi, and Sarasvati. Though the Goddess is one, She is represented and worshiped in three different aspects. On the first three nights of the festival, Durga is worshiped. Lakshmi is worshiped on the next three nights, and then Sarasvati Devi on the last three nights. The following day, the tenth day of the festival, is called Vijayadasami. *Vijaya* means "victory," the victory over our own minds that can come only when we have worshiped these three: Durga, Lakshmi, and Sarasvati.

Durga

To gain noble virtues, all evil tendencies in the mind must be destroyed. This destruction is represented by Goddess Durga. Durga is *durgati hariṇī*: "She who removes our evil tendencies." This is why She is called Mahishasura Mardini, the destroyer of *Mahiṣa asura* (demon), *mahiṣa* meaning "buffalo." Isn't there a buffalo in our minds as well?

The buffalo stands for *tamoguṇa*, the quality of laziness, darkness, ignorance, and inertia. We have all these qualities of laziness too. We love to sleep. Although we may have a lot of energy and potential inside us, we prefer to do nothing—just like the buffalo that loves only to lie in pools of water. In the Puranic story, Durga Devi's killing of the Mahisha demon is, symbolically, the destruction of the *tamoguṇa* within us that is very difficult to destroy. In the *Durgā Devī Havana* (sacrifice), we invoke that divine Power within us to destroy our animalistic tendencies.

Lakshmi

For knowledge to dawn within us, we have to prepare our minds. The mind must be pure, concentrated, and single-pointed; this purification of the mind is obtained through worship of Lakshmi Devi.

In our society today, however, when we think of Lakshmi, we think only of money—counting gold and dollar bills! This is why if one goes to a Lakshmi temple, one will find a crowd. Everybody likes *Lakṣmī Pūjā* (*Lakṣmī* worship) because they think She represents material wealth. But what is real wealth? Even if we have material wealth but have no self-discipline or self-control, nor the values of love, kindness, respect, and sincerity, all our material wealth will be lost or destroyed. The real wealth is the inner wealth of spiritual values that we practice in our lives, by which our minds become purified. Only when we have these noble values will we be able to preserve our material wealth and make good use of it. Otherwise, money itself becomes a problem.

In the Upanishads, the rishis never asked for material wealth only. In the mantras of the *Taittirīya Upaniṣad*, they first asked to have all the noble virtues fully developed in themselves. "Having gained the noble virtues, thereafter Lord please bring wealth to us." The rishis express here that in the absence of right values and good qualities, all our money will be wasted. We know this is true because, for example, if we give money to a drug addict or an alcoholic, he will drink or smoke it away in no time.

Our wealth of virtues is our true Lakshmi. Its importance is shown by the fact that Adi Shankaracharya himself, in *Vivekacūḍāmaṇi*, describes the *ṣaṭ sampati*, or six forms of wealth (calmness of mind, self-control, self-withdrawal, forbearance, faith, and single-pointedness) that are to be cultivated to attain wisdom. These virtues are important because our goal is victory over the mind—a victory such that we do not get disturbed by every change that takes place in our lives. This victory comes only when the mind is prepared, and this mental preparation is the symbolism of the *Lakṣmī Pūjā*.

Sarasvati

Victory over the mind can be gained only through knowledge, through understanding; and it is Goddess Sarasvati who represents this highest knowledge of the Self.

Although there are many kinds of knowledge in the Vedas—phonetics, astronomy, archery, architecture, economics, and so on—the real knowledge is spiritual knowledge. Lord Krishna Himself says in the *Bhagavad Gītā*: "The knowledge of the Self is *the* Knowledge"; and He adds, "it is My vibhuti, My glory." In other words, we may have knowledge of many other subjects and sciences, but if we do not know our own Self, then that is the greatest loss. Therefore, the supreme Knowledge is the knowledge of the Self that is represented by Goddess Sarasvati.

Thus, at Navaratri, Goddess Durga is invoked first to remove impurities from the mind. Then Goddess Lakshmi is invoked to cultivate the noble values and qualities. Finally, Sarasvati is invoked for gaining the highest knowledge of the Self. This is the significance of the three sets of three nights, and when all these three are gained subjectively, then there will be Vijayadasami, the day of true victory!

At Navaratri time, the *rasa* dance (the dance of joy) of Sri Krishna and the *gopīs* is also performed. As the mind becomes purer, calmer, quieter, and more cheerful, and greater understanding is gained, do we not feel happier? Similarly, the *rasa* is the dance of joy—the joy of realization. But nowadays, the theme of Sri Krishna and the *gopīs* dancing the *rasa* has been lost in our society. Today the true meaning and purpose of the ritual is forgotten, as more importance is given to other types of dancing.

Why is the Navaratri festival celebrated at night rather than in the daytime? This is another interesting question. Nighttime is generally the time when we go to sleep, so the spiritual message of nighttime worship is: "You have lived long enough in the sleepy ignorance of *tamoguṇa*. It is time to get up now. Please, wake up!"

For a *pūjā*, unfortunately, we are never willing to stay up late and so we ask, "What time will it end?" For a party, we never ask this question. If the party ends at 10:00 pm, we say, "What! The party is finished?! What kind of a party is that?!" Yet we find it difficult to stay awake for a *pūjā*!

The Importance of Ritual

Not everyone, it is true, will be of the intellectual type to appreciate everything philosophically. Therefore, philosophy or spiritual truth must be demonstrated visually in some ritualistic form. In this way, when children are first introduced to it, they enjoy a dance or a festival, and then later on begin to question, "What is this dance? Why are we doing this *pūjā*? What is the meaning of Navaratri?" So the purpose of the concretized ritual is fulfilled when these questions begin to arise in the children's minds.

Unfortunately, when we take our children to functions at the temples and they begin to ask questions about what they see, we cannot answer them. Yet when the children revolt later as teenagers, we say, "What happened to the children? These kids are terrible. We never used to question our religion!"

We take pride in the fact that we never used to question anything, but it would have been better if we had asked questions and found out. Why did we not ask? Because of intellectual inertia. Inertia is of different kinds. Physical inertia is not as bad because it is usually temporary. There are also mental or emotional stupors that some people remain in, but the intellectual inertia is the worst kind because under its influence, we do not want to think at all. It is said that people can live without air for two minutes, without water for a few days, without food for a month or so, and without thinking for *generations*! Some people just do not want to think. This is our inner Mahisha, and our spiritual Mahisha is that we do not want to wake up from this sleep of ignorance.

As we can see, the theme of the entire Vedas is reflected in the Navaratri festival: Purify the mind and remove all negativities; cultivate positive virtues; gain spiritual knowledge and transcend limitations. This is the real victory—the dance of joy—ritualistically performed at night, as it is on Shivaratri (auspicious night), to signify our spiritual awakening.

The Three Subdivisions of Each Veda

When we come to the Vedas, we will find a corresponding theme of spiritual development, as explained in the Navaratri festival.

Each Veda contains three portions: the *karma kāṇḍa*; which we generally translate as the "ritualistic portion" and that entails much more than mere rituals; the second portion, called *upāsana kāṇḍa*, which deals with worship and meditation on different aspects of the Lord as we see Him manifested in various forms in the universe; and the third portion, called *jñāna kāṇḍa*, which reveals the highest Knowledge. If we happen to read somewhere that there are only two portions of the Vedas rather than three, then it means that the *upāsana kāṇḍa* is considered to be included in the *karma kāṇḍa* section.

Why are there three portions of the Vedas? Because human beings have three kinds of problems: impurities of the mind, restlessness of the mind, and ignorance of the Self. Ignorance, in fact, is the cause for the other two problems.

Is our mind not wandering and restless all the time? Why is this? It is due to impurity. Though we do not like to hear this word, what does it really mean? Let us try to understand it by looking at our lives.

Throughout our lives, we perform actions and receive various results. We meet different people and go through many experiences and circumstances. Yet all these activities can be classified into two categories: perception and response. We perceive an object or interpret a situation; then we act upon or within the situation, which is followed by a result. This result we must either suffer or enjoy, and then again respond. This, in short, is the cycle of our lives: perception and response.

But the question is: How are we perceiving and responding? What is the motivating factor behind these actions? Are all our responses really objective, or are they prejudiced and preconditioned?

When we perform actions, are they really performed in the knowledge of what is right or wrong, or are they according to our whims and fancies?

If we analyze ourselves, we will find that we readily do those things that we like to do, but when it comes to doing things we do not like, we start justifying ourselves saying, "I am a rational, intelligent being; why should I have to do this?" It is not that we really want to understand why we should perform the action or duty, but that we are in the habit of questioning those things we do not want to do.

For example, when we ask a youngster to attend a spiritual function, he may say, "Why should I?" Yet in his own circle he gives into peer pressure. He may insist on wearing jeans with a hole here and a hole there, without ever having stopped to question himself. In short, if he wants to do it he will do it, and only when he does not want to do something will he ask questions. This is true with a child, a youngster, or an adult of any caste, creed, or nationality.

Then what is the motivating factor behind doing things we like to do and avoiding things we do not like to do? In technical, scriptural language, our activities are said to be *vāsanā anusāri*, "prompted by our inherent tendencies (*vāsanās*)," that manifest in the form of likes and dislikes.

Think about it: Whenever we meet a new person, do we really look at him objectively, or do we already have likes and dislikes in our mind concerning him? "Oh, he is Muslim, he must be like this"; or, "He is an American, he must be like that." All our perceptions, actions, and responses are controlled by our likes (*rāga*) and our dislikes (*dveṣa*), which are direct manifestations of our *vāsanās*. These likes and dislikes are what we call the impurities of the mind.

What, then, is the result of this type of behavior? The more we act and react according to our *vāsanās*, the stronger they become. Thus the *vāsanās* become even more deeply rooted. As the *Bhagavad Gītā* says:

> *The branches of that tree of* saṃsāra *(transmigration), extending*

> *downward and upward, are strengthened by the* guṇas *(qualities) and have sense objects as their shoots. And the roots that are followed by actions, spread downward in the human world.* (XV:2)

In this metaphor, our life in the world is compared with a banyan tree with secondary roots that go down and get deeply rooted in the earth. In the same way, we get pulled down and rooted deeply in the world of illusion by our *vāsanās*. The more we follow their dictates, the stronger they become. We ourselves feed the strength of the *vāsanās*. Take, for instance, the habit of smoking: The more we continue smoking, the stronger the habit becomes. This is true of tea, coffee, alcohol, or anything else; by repetition of the action, the habit becomes stronger.

The impurities of the mind must be eliminated, and this is the purpose of the *karma kāṇḍa* portion of the Vedas. The mind is restless because of innumerable likes and dislikes that cause the mind to run from one direction to another and from one object to another. Consequently, it is not available for knowledge. To the extent the mind becomes pure, it becomes steady and concentrated.

Occasionally people can force the mind to concentrate for some time, but if the mind is not purified, whatever power is gained as a result of their concentration will ultimately be misused by them. That is why it is said that power corrupts and absolute power corrupts absolutely! It all depends on the quality of the mind.

In the *Tulsī Rāmāyaṇa* it is said that when Bharata gained the kingdom, in the sense that he agreed to rule only as a regent during Sri Ramachandra's absence, he came to meet Sri Rama at Chitrakuta. Lakshmana doubted Bharata's motive and thought that since he had gained a powerful position, it must have gone to his head and he would want to defeat Sri Rama. Assuming that Bharata had become corrupt, Lakshmana wanted to fight with him; but Sri Rama told Lakshmana that power only corrupts those who are impure in mind and those who have never associated themselves with holy people in *satsaṅga* (the company of holy people). But, Sri Rama added, Bharata himself is such a great saint that he does not need to have *satsaṅga*, and other people will be purified just by living near him.

In conclusion, then, our goal is to purify our minds, and the *karma kāṇḍa* portion of the Vedas has been given to us for this purpose. How *karma*, or work, accomplishes this goal of mental purification will be the topic of our next chapter.

IV

The Karma Kāṇḍa

Hindu culture is essentially a Vedic culture, called *Vaidika Saṃskṛti*, since it is based on the authority of the Vedas. The subject matter of the Vedas is classified into three parts: the *karma kāṇḍa* (ritualistic portion); the *upāsanā kāṇḍa* (worship portion); and the *jñāna kāṇḍa* (knowledge portion).

The Vedas point out that the purpose of human life is to realize and to know the absolute Truth, the absolute Reality, and not just to live superficially in the world of appearances. In order to know this Truth the mind must be prepared and purified, and so the first portion of the Vedas, the *karma kāṇḍa*, is meant for acquiring this purity of mind.

When we act and respond in this world to different situations and experiences, our actions and responses tend not to be objective. They are often prejudiced, colored, and conditioned by our personal likes and dislikes, which are expressions of our *vāsanās*, the subtle impressions and inherent tendencies gathered in innumerable lifetimes. When we act, prompted by our *vāsanās*, rather than guided by the knowledge of what is right and wrong, we strengthen these likes and dislikes, which constitute the impurities of mind.

Daily Disciplines

How can we purify the mind? The answer is provided in the *karma kāṇḍa*, or ritualistic portion of the Vedas. We will see, in fact, that the mental purity attained through the *karma kāṇḍa* is directly related to the single-pointedness that is attained through the *upāsana* portion of the Vedas. For when the mind is full of impurities with many likes and dislikes, desire, anger, and passion, then the mind will also be agitated by those emotions. On the other hand, to the extent that the mind is pure, it will be calm and single-pointed. Let us now see how *karma* achieves this goal of mental purity for us.

Most people have the idea that the *karma kāṇḍa* refers only to rituals, *homas*, *havanas*, *yajñas*, or *pūjās*, and so we become frightened by the word and wonder, "How am I going to do all these rituals?" But this is an incomplete and superficial understanding. In the *karma kāṇḍa* different kinds of *karmas*, or actions, are prescribed for different purposes. These types of *karmas* or rituals are called *kāmya karmas*, actions prompted by a desire to get a particular result, and are therefore done by choice.

For example, some rituals are given for the attainment of heaven: "Let him who has a desire for heaven perform the *Jyotiṣṭoma* sacrifice." Other sacrifices are for the attainment of wealth or for conceiving children, such as the *putreṣṭi yajña* that King Dasharatha performed. These rituals are meant for the fulfillment of particular desires and are only required if one has a desire for a particular object. Otherwise, these rituals are obsolete. If I have no desire to go to heaven, I am not required to perform a sacrifice for its attainment, just as there is no need for an Indian to apply for an American visa if he does not want to go to America.

Another type of *karma* or ritual is called *nitya karma*. According to our respective stage in life, a duty is assigned to us which we are to perform daily for the discipline of the mind. For instance, a *brahmacārī* (student) must do *gāyatrī japa* as a daily duty. The householder, the *vānaprastha* (one who has retired from worldly activities for spiritual pursuits), and the *sannyāsī* (renunciate) are all given particular daily duties. These duties are meant to bring discipline into our lives because we are, at this moment, very indisciplined in our actions.

"Indisciplined" means "licentious." We sleep whenever we want, we wake up when we want to wake up, and we eat at any time whether we are hungry or not. If we see things on sale we purchase them whether we need them or not. We indulge in many things just because they are available.

Today this Vedic culture is little known, and it is only rarely that the grandparents can pass the tradition on to the grandchildren. Many parents also do not know the cultural and religious traditions, and whatever little values the children gather they absorb only through *Sesame Street*! It is very interesting to note that television has become the guru! Instead of *ācārya devo bhava* (consider the Guru as God), we have gone to *dūradarśana devo bhava* (consider the television as God). In Sanskrit, television would be *dūradarśana* since *dūra* means "far" and *darśana* means "vision."

On some of these programs children are taught to have consideration for others, to be accommodating, and not to fight with each other. But the after-school programs for teenagers are completely different and they learn to think, "Why should I have consideration for anyone else? I have my own individuality." So, all the values of brotherhood which the children learned earlier are lost as they grow up.

The main point is that there should be discipline in our lives, and in order to teach our children, we ourselves must undergo some discipline. For instance, our parents with whom we lived in India might have established the rule that unless you bathe first, no tea will be given to you; or before you prostrate to the Lord at the altar, you will not be given any food—some discipline, whatever it might be.

If, for example, as soon as you wake up in the morning you have a desire for a cup of coffee, but you make the rule that unless you do at least one *mālā* (rosary) of *japa* you will not have the coffee, this in itself will be a great accomplishment. If you can keep at least one of these disciplines in your life, the mind will slowly come under your control. In any and all of these disciplines, we are slowly learning to control our urges. This is the important thing.

So whereas the *kāmya karmas* are performed out of choice by the person who has a desire for a particular object, *nitya karmas* are daily disciplines required according to our stage in life, whether we are students, householders, retired persons, or renunciates. We are told that we must abide by these disciplines meticulously and that only under extraordinary situations are we to relax them.

But what is happening in our case is just the opposite. For instance, we are allowed to sleep more if we are especially exhausted or ill, but only occasionally do we decide to get up early to do some special activity or worship. In other words, only now and then do we decide to follow the rule; so that which is the exception has become the rule for us, and that which is supposed to be the rule has become the exception! This is why our willpower is not strong and when we cannot follow even a simple discipline, we find it impossible to face bigger challenges and we start cursing ourselves. But when we perform some discipline regularly we find that our willpower is strengthened in many ways.

Let us take a simple example. Suppose we decide to get up regularly at four or five o'clock in the morning. Then we will also have to go to sleep early, and if we go to sleep early, we have to eat earlier and have only light food. Also, television watching or whatever other activity we continue to do until late at night will be reduced. Aside from this, if we rise early in the morning, we can work without any disturbance and we find so much extra time available.

Thus even if we are able to keep one discipline in our lives and make it a rule for ourselves, many other aspects also become disciplined and under our control. By this *nitya karma* we slowly gain mastery and control over our minds.

Duties Enjoined by Others

The third type of *karma* is called *kartavya karma*, meaning duties enjoined on us by others, such as parents, teachers, the government, or by our place of employment. A youngster may reject his parents' rules and refuse to obey them, but when he goes to find a job at a restaurant, he will have to obey the boss. Though he may not wash his own cup or plate at home, at the restaurant he will have to wash everybody's dishes! Otherwise he will be fired! Similarly, even though we may revolt in one place, no matter where we go there will be some duty we must fulfill. In fact it is the effort or sincerity with which one tries to fulfill his or her duties that we really respect.

If we start our own business or industry and employ many people, what is it that we expect from others? Do we not expect everybody to be obedient and disciplined? Will we tolerate or allow any employee to continue if he is inefficient, indisciplined, lazy, or not punctual? Some people think that money alone is everything, but we really respect only these higher values and good qualities such as sincerity, honesty, and punctuality in each other.

The problem is that we want and expect these values to be in others, but not in ourselves. We may earn money by any means fair or foul, but we want our accountant to be honest; we expect our employees or servants to be sincere and honest even if we are not. These higher values are what we really respect and admire.

Success comes only to a person who is well disciplined in his life, for without discipline no success is possible. All the problems of the world could be solved if only each person started thinking, "Let me cultivate and have all these good values in myself." This is very important. But we are so used to problems now that if suddenly there are no more problems we are frightened and think, "What will I do now?"

The Vedas tell us to be steadfast in our duties whether they are only simple, daily duties or duties enjoined on us by others. Do not consider what others are doing or not doing; be only concerned about fulfilling your own duty. There are some who say, "Why should I do this work? I am the only one doing my duty and no one else is doing his." But if we become ill, do we wait for the other person to go to the doctor first saying, "I will not go to the doctor until he does!" No, whether the other person goes or not, we know that we must get well and so we go to the doctor for treatment.

In the same way, here we want to gain spiritual health, our true natural health. Therefore, in the performance of duty, we should not care whether another person is working or not. Also, in the fulfillment of duty, the question of likes and dislikes should not arise. We must have the attitude that we do this work because it has to be done.

Thus the first portion of the Vedas advocates the taking up of daily discipline and doing it consistently without compromise. Whatever duties are enjoined on us, whether at home or at work, we must remain steadfast in them. We are also instructed to slowly reduce our desire-prompted activities and the constant expectation of "What will I get?"

Of course we should also not indulge in prohibited *karmas*, meaning actions that are below our human dignity, such as stealing or killing. Prohibited actions are generally motivated by desires that force us to do anything to anybody to satisfy the desire.

Scriptural Injunctions

In the *karma kāṇḍa* portion of the Vedas, there are many types of instructions: "Do this. Do not do that." But we are very allergic to these. If anyone says, "Do this," we say, "Why should I?" and if we are told "Do not do this," we say, "Why not?" We do just the opposite of what we are told. This is a meaningless revolt, however.

Once there was a boy who was taught about the Ten Commandments and was told that anyone who disobeyed the Commandments would go to hell. Then someone asked the little boy, "Do you know what will happen if you break one of the Ten Commandments?" The little boy replied, "Nine will remain!"

The point is that when we are given so many rules and regulations to follow, we feel that we are being bound and restricted by our parents, teachers, society, or by the government. But if we go to the scriptures and ask, "Why are you giving us all these injunctions and commandments; why are you binding us?" The rishis (seers) and the Vedas reply, "We are not binding you because you are already bound by all your likes and dislikes, desires, and anger. We are actually releasing you from your bondage."

It is something like this: I was suffering from high blood pressure and went to the doctor. The doctor told me to stop eating pickles.

I said, "Stop eating pickles? That is what tickles my tongue most! I like it very much!" He said, "No, you stop eating pickles, papad, and other fried things. Only eat bland food." The doctor gave me all kinds of "dos" and "don'ts" about what to eat and not to eat. I said, "Doctor, with all your instructions, you are making me sick!" He said, "You are already sick! I am giving you all these instructions so that if you follow them closely, you will enjoy good health again and will be able to eat normally!"

By their prescriptions, therefore, the medical doctors are not making us sick, rather they are relieving us of our sickness. Similarly the rishis in our scriptures are our spiritual doctors, who, by their many instructions, are actually relieving us of our spiritual illness.

In fact, we will find these "dos" and "don'ts" wherever we go—even on goods that we purchase we receive instructions—so that we may make good use of all our equipments. When it comes to ourselves, however, we immediately revolt. This revolt is meaningless, however, because if we understand the purpose behind scriptural injunctions and remain steadfast in self-discipline and duty, we will see our minds becoming calm, pure, and single-pointed.

My purpose is just to give you an insight into the subject matter of the Vedas, but you can study the details more for yourself later. Thus in general, we have seen so far: the *kāmya karmas*—actions performed in order to gain a particular result; the *nitya karmas*—daily disciplines; and the *kartavya karmas*—duties imposed upon us by others, which we must fulfill as long as we are benefiting from society.

Purification Rituals

Another kind of ritual performed as a purificatory act is called *saṃskāra karma*. These rituals are seen everywhere, throughout every individual's life. In the Vedic age there was a ritual performed at the birth of a child, and later when he went to the school or *gurukula*, the sacred thread ceremony was performed. When school-life ended, a convocation ceremony called the *samāvartana* was performed for graduation. Though many people are now protesting against these kinds of rituals, we are only replacing them with all our modern social rituals, are we not?

In America there are graduation ceremonies even at the primary school level. I was surprised to find this out because in India even for post-graduate students only a certificate is given; family members do not go to see the ceremony.

When I came to America for the second time and gave a program in Michigan, a couple said to me, "Swamiji, we will not be able to come to your talk tomorrow."

I said, "Why? What is the problem?"

They said, "Tomorrow we have to go to a graduation ceremony."

I thought it must be for some university student and asked, "Who is it for and for what?"

They replied, "It is for our nephew who is graduating from high school."

I said, "For a high school graduation? What is so great about that?"

And they said to me, "Oh Swamiji, you do not know! Only when you live here will you understand what a big thing it is."

Now I know that if the parents do not go to that ceremony, they have had it!

As you can see, these graduation ceremonies are big rituals in themselves, just like many other occasions that are celebrated such as: birthdays, Mother's Day, Father's Day, Valentine's Day, Independence Day, and so on. The marriage ceremony is also an important ritual, in which two individuals promise, in front of other people, that they are accepting each other and their responsibilities as husband and wife. Similarly, when a person is elected president and must go through the inaugural ceremony, is this not again a ritual?

Why do we engage in these rituals? Because in the performance of the ritual, an impression is left upon the mind of the person or persons involved so that they feel they are beginning a new life and have a new responsibility to fulfill. When the president takes the oath, he feels, "Now I have a big responsibility. The nation is looking up to me and I must guide it as best as I can."

This impression left on the mind as a result of the ritual is called *saṃskāra vidhi*.

Thus we have seen the various *karmas* or types of action prescribed by the *karma kāṇḍa* portion of the Vedas: *kāmya karma*, *nitya karma*, *kartavya karma*, and *saṃskāra karma*. We have also discussed their purposes: the purification, discipline, and control of the mind, and impressing upon it a higher sense of duty and responsibility toward others—beyond mere personal sense gratification.

The Upasana Kāṇḍa

The second portion of the Vedas is the *upāsana kāṇḍa*. *Upāsana* means "worship" or, literally, "sitting near." *Upa* means "near," and *āsana* means "sitting." Now "sitting near" is not meant only in the physical sense so that if I am doing *guru upāsana*, I must only sit next to the guru. It means that we must sit mentally near the object of our worship, and when we do this, we begin to slowly imbibe the qualities of that object.

The best example is a log of wood when it is placed near a fire. The log gradually becomes heated up and catches fire. For the log of wood this would be called *agni upāsana* (sitting near the fire). Similarly, if I am cold and sit near a fire, I will also feel the heat of the fire and become warm.

In the same way, in the Vedas, it is said that we must do the *iṣṭadevatā upāsana* (the worship of our chosen deity). Nowadays we also have Rama, Krishna, and Shiva as idols for worship. In truth, these are not mere idols, but ideals. As Swami Chinmayananda says, every idol represents an ideal.

People unnecessarily criticize idol worship because they do not understand its significance. But in one form or another, everyone does idol worship. What are we doing when we salute the national flag? Though we see only a piece of cloth, we are really saluting or revering the ideal which the flag represents—our national aspirations, our values, our entire culture. Because the flag symbolizes something greater than a piece of cloth, people protesting against a particular nation burn the flag of that country.

Once an American was talking to a Dutchman, and the American asked the Dutchman, "What is your national flag?"

The Dutchman replied, "There are just three stripes on it, red, white, and blue."

"What do they represent?" asked the American.

"Nothing special," said the Dutchman. "They just represent our country at the time of tax collection. When we hear that it is time for taxes, our faces get red; when we think about how much we have to pay, our faces turn white; and when we actually pay the money to the government, our faces turn blue! So these colors are the three conditions of our faces at tax-time. And what about your flag?"

The American replied, "Ours is the same. The only difference is that at tax time we also see stars!"

This story is simply to illustrate that one can always ascribe other meanings to the physical symbols that we use. Who then does not perform idol worship in one form or another?

The use of symbols for worship is meant for making our minds single-pointed, whereby we gain the very same qualities of the ideal we revere. This is just like tuning our television to a particular channel; we receive whatever program is being broadcast by that station.

A devotee meditating on Sri Ramachandra, who was the model of a perfect king, son, husband, and brother, will slowly gain those same qualities as Sri Rama.

Similarly, we also become exactly like the company we keep. For instance, a person who was not a smoker before started living with people who smoked all the time, and they said, "Why do you not smoke also?" So he thought, "Why not try it just once?" and after that he became a regular smoker! This can be called smoke *upāsana*! There can be many other kinds of *upāsanas*: drink *upāsana*, dance *upāsana*, and so on. When we live in the company of people who do these things, we slowly imbibe those same qualities and tendencies.

In the *upāsana* portion of the Vedas, wonderful meditations are prescribed, in which we are given a *pratīka*, a symbol representing a greater ideal, upon which to fix the mind. By gathering all our attention at one point, we gain all the virtues of that ideal and finally become one with it. When the mind is thus purified, sharpened, and made single-pointed, it becomes a powerhouse of energy, and with such dynamism anything can be achieved. The culmination of our practice of the *karma-* and *upāsana-kāṇḍas* is the readiness of the mind for the highest Knowledge—the knowledge of the Self.

What is contained in this last and most important portion of the Vedas, the *jñāna kāṇḍa*, will be discussed in our next chapter.

V

The Jñāna Kāṇḍa

When our minds are purified through *karma* (selfless action) and made single-pointed through *upāsana* (worship), we cannot remain satisfied with the small achievements in worldly life. We begin to ask questions, such as: "What is the purpose of life? What is my true nature? What is this world and from where has it come? What is the source and origin of this entire creation?"

When questions of this kind arise in a person's mind, his or her quest for knowledge begins. This quest can be satisfied only when the student approaches a spiritual master and learns from him this highest Knowledge of the Self. This Knowledge is the subject matter of the third and last portion of the Vedas, which we call the Upanishads, otherwise known as Vedanta.

When we say "Vedanta" philosophy, we mean the knowledge that is revealed in the Upanishads. Therefore, we do not have to say that we are studying both the Upanishads and Vedanta because the two words have the same meaning.

The Upanishads

Upaniṣad is a combination of three words: *Upa*, *ni*, and *sad*. *Upa* means "near," *ni* means "below" and "determination," *and sad* means "to sit down." Thus the simple meaning of *Upaniṣad* is "near below sitting." The indicative meaning is that a student, having developed sufficiently good qualities of heart and mind, with a burning desire for knowledge, approaches a teacher, sits at his feet, tunes his mind to the teachings given by the master, and tries his best to absorb and practice the teachings. In short, the Upanishads contain that Knowledge which can be gained by a seeker of Truth when he is sitting at the feet of his spiritual master.

Why is it said that the student must sit at the teacher's feet? Because, just as the flow of water is natural and effortless from an upper to a lower level but not in the other direction, sitting at the feet of the teacher is symbolic of the student looking up to the teacher with respect and reverence. With this attitude of the student, the knowledge of the teacher flows easily to him.

The other meanings of the word *sad* are "to destroy" and "to lead." When the student receives this knowledge from the teacher, his ignorance of the real nature of the world and of his own Self is destroyed. Therefore, the purpose of the Upanishad is *ajñāna nāśa*, the destruction of ignorance. The most important point is that the word "Upanishad" does not, essentially, refer to a book, but to this highest Knowledge, the knowledge of the Self.

The word *ni*, in Sanskrit, also means "determination." This indicates that the student must approach the teacher with a firm determination to gain this Knowledge. He must feel that "unless and until I gain this Knowledge, I am not leaving here." If the teacher tells him that he must first stay in the ashram for a 100 years, the student must be ready to stay. In other words, the student must feel that he is ready to abide by whatever instruction and advice the teacher gives him. A Sanskrit verse says beautifully: *Dehaṃ vā pātayāmi kāryam vā sādayāmi*. "Either this body will fall down dead or I will accomplish my goal." This is the firm determination with which the student has to approach the teacher.

Self-Knowledge

In all the four Vedas there are the three sections of *karma*, *upāsana*, and *jñāna*. The *jñāna* section is comprised of many Upanishads. Even though there are more than 108 Upanishads in the Vedas, the knowledge taught in them is the same: the knowledge of the Self.

What is Self-Knowledge? What is the real subject matter of

the Upanishads? For all of us living here in this world, questions such as, "Who am I, what is this world, and where did it come from?" eventually arise. The first question is related to myself and my own true nature, while the second question relates to the nature of the world that I see around me. Our desire for the knowledge that will answer these questions is fulfilled in the Upanishads. They tell us that *Brahman* is the origin of this creation and is also our own true nature.

The next question we would want to ask is what is *Brahman*? One Upanishad gives two main definitions that make the subject matter clearer. "*Brahman* is that from which all beings are born, that by which they are sustained, and that unto which they return."

The word *Brahman* is not very common, but the word "God" is. Though many people have doubts and questions when they speak of God, there is one thing which all of us, even the scientists, will accept: For every creation, product, or manufactured thing, there must be a cause, a source. When we look at the universal creation as a whole, most everyone agrees that there must be a cause for it. However, when the scriptures call that source God or *Brahman*, some people say, "No, we do not accept that." In other words, the idea of source or origin is acceptable to them, but not when it is referred to as God.

In the Upanishads *Brahman* is said to be, first of all, the source of all creation. Secondly, *Brahman* is also indicated in this way: "That which is not perceived by the eyes as an object, as a color, or a form, but because of which the eyes are able to see. That is *Brahman* [which we call God]."

Again, the *Kena Upaniṣad* says:

> *That which is not seen, but because of which the eyes are able to see; that which cannot be described by words, but because of which our speech is able to describe other things; that which is not heard by the ears, but because of which our ears are able to hear; that is* Brahman. (I: 4-7)

This is a profound definition of God, and if an atheist were to say, "I do not believe in God," we can see that God is That because of whom he was able even to speak the very sentence!

Thus God is pointed out in the Upanishads as pure Consciousness, That because of which we are able to see, to hear, to speak, and because of which we are able to think: "That which is not thought of by the mind, but because of which the mind is able to think—that is *Brahman*." This is our own Self.

Once a person approached Bhagavan Ramana Maharshi and said, "O Bhagavan, can you show me God?" Ramana Maharshi replied, "I can show you, but I do not know whether you will see Him." The man felt insulted and said, "If you can show Him to me, why can I not see Him? I have eyes." He did not realize that one must have more than just physical eyes to see God; one must have true Knowledge. The man insisted, "No, you show me and I will see." So Bhagavan Ramana Maharshi sat in front of him. Then he just raised one finger and started moving it from one side to another. Five, ten, fifteen minutes went by. The man was still expecting some vision of God to appear. Finally, the man asked, "I thought you were going to show me God. Where is He?"

Bhagavan said, "I told you I can show you God, but you may not be able to see Him."

The man said, "But you have not shown me anything."

"For twenty minutes I have been showing you God," Bhagavan said.

"How can that be?" asked the confused man.

Then Bhagavan raised his finger and asked "What is this?"

"A finger."

"But what is it doing?"

"It is moving back and forth," the man replied.

Ramana Maharshi said, "I am showing you God, but you are seeing only a finger. What can I do? That is your problem."

"But," the man protested, "anyone will say it is only a finger!"

Ramana Maharshi replied, "If you cut this finger and put it on the table, does it move?"

"No, it does not move."

"Now, what is it because of which the finger moves?"

"There is life in it," answered the man.

"You see," said Ramana Maharshi, "at most you can say there is life in the finger, but that life is only an expression of Consciousness. Therefore, that which is expressing in this body as life, as sentiency, is God. How can you deny its existence?"

The Highest Achievement

In the light of an electric bulb, we can see many objects in a room, but not electricity itself. That because of which there is light in the bulb is called electrical energy; yet the light itself is not electricity. In the same way, that because of which there is life in this body is called *Brahman*, the Self. Its existence cannot be denied by anyone. Therefore, *Brahman* is said to be the origin of all this creation and is seated in the hearts of all beings as Consciousness. To know that this Consciousness is Me is the highest achievement that a human being can gain. There is nothing greater than this because once we know that it is only the Self which is appearing as this total universe, our sense of limitation and finitude ends and our entire vision of the world changes. When I look out at the same world, my understanding of it will be different; I will see it as my very own Self.

This, in short, is the subject matter of the Upanishads, the *jñāna* portion of the Vedas, which is also called Vedanta. This portion deals with the knowledge of *Brahman* (also known as *Ātman*) and dispels the ignorance about our own true Self. In Sanskrit this knowledge is called *Brahmajñāna* or *Brahmavidyā*. All our efforts in spiritual practices (*sādhanas*), all rituals, temples, idols of gods, and various religious symbols are meant only to lead the individual (*jīva*) to this final realization.

Oneness in Diversity

Now we will touch upon another topic which is found to be confusing to many Hindus as well as to people of other faiths; that is, the notion that Hinduism has many gods.

What are these multiple gods? Are there really many gods in Hinduism? No, the Upanishads are very clear in pointing out that there is only one God, one Truth. In the *Chāndogya Upaniṣad* it is said: "In the beginning, all this was nothing but *Sat* (Existence) alone." And "It is One without a second, *Brahman*."

And what is that One? The Upanishads say that in Itself, the Truth is that which cannot be defined by any words because only a finite thing can be described, never an infinite thing. Therefore, *Brahman* is pointed out as that which is nameless and formless: "That which is not a sound, a taste, a color, or a touch." It is the attributeless, nameless, formless, and pure Existence.

Brahman also has the infinite power to express in many ways, through manifold forms. Let us take an example which will make this concept easier to understand.

We use the word "government" frequently—the government has made this decision, the government is raising taxes, and so on. Everyday we hear or read this on the radio, television, and newspaper. When I was a child I thought that the government was the name of an individual person. But is the government a person or an object with a form that can be seen? What is its color, its taste, or texture? The government cannot be pointed out by any of these terms or qualities as such because the word does not indicate one particular individual in the way the word "president" does.

And where is the government located? As far as this country is concerned, we say that the government is all-pervading, it is everywhere in this nation. If someone says, "Show me where the government is," you cannot do it because the government, as a power, exists everywhere in the nation and cannot be said to exist only in one place. However, we may be able to indicate particular offices where the government officials are located, though it is sometimes difficult to find the officials there, no doubt!

Now, we say in the United States that if you go to Washington, D.C., you will find the government there. This is because there are so many government buildings, offices, secretaries, under secretaries, and so on. Yet all these people put together are not the government; the government is still much more than that. What is seen is only the power of the government expressing and functioning through these innumerable people in government positions.

Just as the government is one, but the government officials are many, it is said there is one supreme Being that is pure Existence, Consciousness—omniscient and omnipotent. It is that Being alone who expresses as different powers and is known by different names. This does not mean that the One has actually become many, just as a broken glass breaks into many pieces. For instance, in myself I am one, yet I also have various powers that are expressing through different mediums. The power within me that expresses through the eyes is called the power of seeing, and when I use this power to see, then I am called a seer. When the same power expresses through my ears it is called the power of hearing and, accordingly, I am called a hearer. Depending on the medium through which my consciousness is functioning, I am also called a taster, toucher, smeller, feeler, thinker, doer, or enjoyer. Now is there really more than one "I"? Though this "I," which is of the nature of pure Consciousness, is really one, it appears to be many when it expresses as different powers functioning through my various sense or mental faculties. But does it mean that I myself have become many?

Again, the powers are said to be many because the mediums through which the one power is expressing are many. This is also true with electrical energy. Electricity is of one homogenous nature, pervading the entire world, but when it functions through the heater, refrigerator, radio, television, or amplifier, its expressions are different. Functioning through the heater, the electrical power is called heat. When the same electrical energy functions through the radio, it expresses as sound. The energy is one and the same, but we call it by different names according to the medium through which it expresses. In the same way, I, the pure Being, the one Power, acquires a different name or status according to its manifestation through either the senses or the mind. The one "I" apparently becomes many: as "I" the speaker, listener, doer, eater, and so on.

In one's relations to other people also, the same entity is referred to in different ways. In relation to my parents I am called son; in relation to my sister, I am called brother; and in relation to my grandparents, I am called grandson.

Once a person was sick and his different relations phoned the doctor. The child called and said, "My daddy is sick, please come." The wife said, "My husband is sick, please come and help." The mother also called and said, "My son is sick, please come and see what is wrong with him." The doctor wondered, "How many people are sick in that house?" But when he came to their home he found that only one person was sick. So the person is one, but he is called by different names according to the different relationships he has. But does he himself become many?

Similarly, that one infinite Being, *Brahman*, acting through its creative power is called the Creator; acting through its sustaining power is called the Sustainer; and acting through its destructive power is called the Destroyer. This does not mean that the Creator, Sustainer, and Destroyer are three separate beings, but that the one same Being is expressing through these three different powers. Just as many laws, departments, regulations, and forces exist in order to control and govern the country, this whole universe is controlled by many laws and forces of nature, and the different deities presiding over them. These deities, again, are not different from the one Lord but are smaller manifestations of the one Power.

In Hinduism, therefore, there are not many gods. All the different forms of Hindu gods and goddesses are but one God expressing in different ways. This one idea should be clear to us and if one studies the Hindu scriptures properly, there will be no doubt concerning it.

Puranic Literature

This basic concept of oneness in diversity is also the underlying foundation of all the Puranic literature though it seems, at first, to be confusing and contradictory. The Puranic literature includes the *Viṣṇu*, *Śiva*, *Brahmāṇḍa*, *Varuṇa*, and *Kūrma Purāṇas*, and other texts pertaining to the stories of particular Hindu deities.

In the *Viṣṇu Purāṇa*, for example, it is said that Lord Vishnu is the supreme Being and that all creation, including all the other gods, have come from Him. When we read the *Ganeṣa Purāṇa*, however, Lord Ganesha is pointed out as the supreme God and from Him Vishnu, Shiva, and Devi have been created. Yet in the *Devī Purāṇa*, it is said that Devi is the Highest and from Her all other gods have come. People become confused when they read this. But the very fact that the *Purāṇa* says that the whole creation has come from one Being means that that which is represented by the words Ganesha, Shiva, or Vishnu is one and the same Reality.

Different forms of the One are recognized in the Hindu religion so that people can worship whichever form attracts them most. Swami Chinmayananda explains that some people can only conceive of God as Master and Ruler, while some can only conceive of God as the Divine Mother. Some worship God as Father, as Friend, or as the divine Beloved. Some people are fond of worshiping God in the form of animals, so there is the form of the elephant-headed god in Hinduism (Ganesha).

Four Aspects of Deity

When we say Shiva, Vishnu, Ganesha, or Devi, there are actually four aspects of the Divinity that can be understood.

For example, Lord Vishnu's first and absolute aspect is the nameless, formless, and attributeless Reality, the origin of this creation. His second identity is as God, the Creator and Sustainer of this world. In fact, the role of sustainer is emphasized more for Lord Vishnu because the name itself means "that which sustains or pervades the entire world." The third identity of Lord Vishnu is as He appears in many different incarnations (*avatāras*) on earth: Vamana, Sri Rama, or Sri Krishna. In these, a particular embodied form as well as special divine activities (*līlās*) are attributed to Him. The fourth aspect is the *iṣṭa rūpa*, the form of that particular deity chosen by the devotee as his favorite for personal worship. In this aspect, Lord Vishnu is most often shown lying on the serpent-bed (*Ananta-Śeṣa*) or standing on a lotus-flower holding conch, discus, mace, and lotus in His four hands.

Thus Lord Vishnu has first His formless aspect as the supreme, infinite Reality; then His cosmic form as the Creator and Sustainer of the world; His third aspect is as a particular incarnation; and fourthly, His form as chosen by the devotee for worship and contemplation.

Lord Shiva's absolute nature as the nameless and formless Reality is the same as Vishnu's and Devi's, as well as of all the other gods and goddesses of Hinduism. In His cosmic form, however, Lord Shiva is represented as the destroyer of the world, playing His *tāṇḍava* drum and dancing in a circle of flames. Thirdly, He is shown in His many incarnations or *avatāras*, assuming different forms, at different times, for different purposes. Lord Shiva is most often said to take *Guru avatāras* (incarnations as a guru, or spiritual master), as Sri Dakshinamurti and Adi Shankaracharya were regarded to be. Lastly, a particular *rūpa* (form) of the deity is given to us for worship, called the arch *avatāra*. In this aspect, Lord Shiva is most often pictured as sitting in meditation with the divine river Ganga, representing Knowledge, flowing down from His head.

Every aspect of a deity's chosen form also has a symbolic meaning and is meant for meditation (*dhyāna*), for which there is always an accompanying meditational verse, called a *dhyāna śloka*. Part of a famous *dhyāna śloka* for Lord Vishnu is:

> I worship Lord Vishnu, Who is the peaceful one, sleeping on the serpent-bed, from Whose navel a lotus grows, Who is the Lord of all the gods, the support of the universe, Who appears to be unlimited like the sky, Who is dark like the rain clouds, and of an auspicious form.

Meditation on the Lord's form enables us to go beyond the form to reach the formless, absolute nature of God. If we do not have this understanding regarding the many forms of the one Reality, even a Hindu can become confused. This happened to one gentleman who complained to me, "Swamiji, I went to Badrinath and bought the respective deity's picture there. I went to Kedarnath and bought that deity's picture also. Then I went to the Meenakshi temple and bought the Meenakshi idol. Now there are so many pictures and idols of gods and goddesses in my meditation room that it is a problem. I have to chant a mantra for each one of them, but if I do that, it will take me two hours and I will be late for work. What should I do?"

I said to him, "Do not worry. Just chose one idol, keep it in front of you, and worship that one."

But the man protested, "Oh, no! If I do that, all the other gods will be angry with me!"

"All right," I said, "you worship half of them in the morning and half of them in the evening!"

This shows how we can create a problem when we do not have the proper understanding. Besides, who asks us to collect idols of gods from all the different temples in the first place?

From the explanation I have given on the Upanishads it should now be clear that, in Hinduism, there is one God or supreme Reality, which manifests or expresses Itself through various powers represented by the forms of different gods and goddesses. Thus there should be no confusion regarding the apparent multiplicity of gods in Hinduism.

PART TWO

The Language of Symbolism

In our sacred books,
the insistence is upon the seeker's mind
constantly lifting itself in attunement
with the ideal of his heart.

Swami Chinmayananda

In every country it is a general practice to have monuments representing great national heroes. These monuments act as reminders and inspire the generations to live up to the ideals set by these heroes. Since ours is a spiritual culture, drawing sustenance and strength from the spiritual ideals lived and demonstrated by the *avatāras*, it is our tradition to preserve and cherish the sacred idols of *avatāras* in temples, for the idols represent the ideals they lived. Temples served as holy halls of retreat for the masses. Their architecture provided an effective medium where the creative arts were fostered, and education for the cultural revival of the country was made available.

As a devotee visits a temple and in a true spirit of devotion, kindled by the Epics and Puranas, is inspired by the vision of the idol he feels a thrill of joy and inner peace, in spite of the prevailing tensions around. It need hardly be emphasized how much more temples are necessary these days. They would serve as "speed-breakers" to soften our hectic blind rush forward in life. They would also serve as sources of inspiration and solace during times of depression and disappointments, which are mostly beyond our control. Building of temples was, therefore, considered as a sacred activity in ancient times, as sacred as any other community service.

Swami Chinmayananda

VI

The Need for Symbols

What is the need for religious symbols? What is the need for the temple? We will now examine these questions. Many of us say that if God is all-pervading, why do we need to have temples? Why should we ever go to one?

The need depends upon the individual person. If you can calculate mathematical formulas mentally, then you have no need of a calculator or pencil and paper. Nowadays, however, most of us are so used to calculators that we cannot even mentally count two plus two! Since we no longer have the self-confidence that we can compute mentally, we need the calculator even more. In the same way, if a person can walk on his own two legs, there is no need for support of crutches or a stick. But a baby, who has neither the strength nor the knowledge of how to stand and balance, requires some support.

Just as some people need support at the physical level, many also require support at the mental and intellectual levels. This is true today even in high-level management courses, where the method of instruction is primarily through visual means of graphs, charts, videos, slide shows, and so on.

Why do we need all these pictures? Why can we not understand a principle by itself without any pictorial demonstration? When a principle or theory is taught to us we generally ask for an illustration or an example to help us understand it better because without it, we feel we cannot comprehend the idea. This is due to our intellectual inability.

On the other hand, if our mind is subtle enough to understand a concept directly, we do not need the help of a symbol. Therefore, the requirement for an outer symbol to convey a subtler idea is not absolute for everyone; it all depends on our qualifications.

But how will we become so highly qualified spiritually that we will not need an outer symbol to help us in our understanding? It is very easy to say that God is all-pervading and formless, but are we really able to meditate on that formless Reality? We may say that God is in every being and thing, but what is the quality of our behavior with other persons when we interact with them? If we say that there is divinity in us and we really see that same divinity in everyone, will we continue to cheat others? It is useless merely to say that God is all-pervading if our behavior remains vulgar and thoughtless. We should not try to fool ourselves.

Certainly it is true that God is all-pervading and that He does not remain only in one image or place, but the question is whether we realize and experience that Truth. If we do not experience it, what is the use in just spewing out a theory? If one already has the direct, living experience that God is formless and all-pervading, one has no need of a temple or an idol, a symbol or a picture. For most of us, however, there is still the need for the support of a symbol in order to prepare the mind—to make it subtle, pure, and capable of seeing the highest Truth. It is for this reason that, if we are not yet able to see the Lord in everything, we are asked to first practice seeing Him in at least one image and then to slowly expand our vision.

Invoking the Awareness of God

Another point that people miss when they criticize others who go to the temple is the fact that if God is all-pervading, then He must be equally present in the temple, in the idol—everywhere! We are, therefore, not worshiping the stone idol, but the presence of God, who is within that form. The temple and the idol are there simply to help bring into our minds an awareness of the presence of God.

Similarly, many people keep a picture of their family in their offices or in their purses. Why do they do this? Not because they think they will forget their dear ones, but because the picture invokes the love they feel for their family and it brings the presence of those loved ones into their minds.

Some people even save a thread or a hair of someone they love. For them it invokes all the memories of love and joy associated with their beloved, though to another person that hair is merely a hair. This is also a kind of idol worship.

It is said that Swami Vivekananda once visited a king who was an atheist and who did not believe in any kind of idol worship. The king said that an idol was just a piece of paper or a stone and to worship it was useless.

In his royal palace there were many pictures of the king's forefathers hanging on the wall. When Swami Vivekananda came he asked one of the ministers to take down the picture of the king's grandfather and put it on the floor. Then he ordered the minister to trample on the picture and spit on it. The king was shocked. He said, "What are you telling him to do?"

Swami Vivekananda repeated, "I told him to spit on that photograph!"

The king was indignant, "What are you saying? How can you insult my grandfather like that!"

"What is wrong?" asked Swami Vivekananda innocently. "It is only a picture. It is not your grandfather, is it?"

Then suddenly the king understood what Swami Vivekananda was driving at and apologized to him for all he had said earlier about idol worship.

For one person a photo may be meaningless, but, as in the example of the king, the picture of the grandfather was more than just a picture. It symbolized the king's whole family ancestry, an ideal that he revered; it represented the man who was the father of his own father, from whom the king had obtained all the property and power now in his possession.

The point is that no matter how insignificant a thing may appear to others, it has the capacity to bring a completely different experience and awareness to the mind of one who is attuned to it. In religion too, as in this worldly type of idol worship, the idol is no mere idol to a devotee, for through it he can come to experience directly the presence of the Lord. Though this experience may not happen immediately, it can certainly come, in time, to a devotee who tunes his mind to, and develops deep love for, that chosen form of the Lord.

In short, the function of the temple and of the idol is to invoke in our minds the awareness of God's presence. Though the form is outside us, the knowledge and awareness takes place within. Becoming aware of God in one place or form is a practice by which we purify the mind and prepare it to understand that this Truth is everywhere and that it is, in fact, our own Self.

The Cultural Role of the Temple

In the Hindu tradition the temple was also meant for another purpose aside from fulfilling the spiritual needs of a person. It was also a place for secular learning, for lectures, for the celebration of special festivals, and for the dedication of music and arts. Whether a person was a painter, sculptor, dancer, or a musician, he could express his or her art in the temple as worship to the Lord. The temples were places where people could come together to share common experiences, not only of a spiritual nature, but also those that were for the total cultural awakening and upliftment of the people—just like our community centers today.

Though recently we have been feeling the need to build modern community buildings and centers for the sake of these various functions, the temples can adequately serve all these purposes, just as they did in earlier days.

Nowadays, since there are rarely any discourses given in the temples, people tend to become overly ritualistic without understanding the meaning of the rituals they perform. Our temples should again become the places where people can learn about their history and culture, their religion and philosophy, as they were originally intended.

The temple also has another deep significance, of which many people are not aware. It is said that structurally the temple represents the human body.

Just as I say that in my body there is the heart (mind or intellect) in which the Lord resides, deep inside the main temple structure is the *garbha gṛha*, the sanctum sanctorum, wherein the Lord's idol presides. The temple itself represents the physical body and the *garbha gṛha* is its heart, wherein we experience the presence of the Lord.

In South Indian temples especially, the whole complex is huge on the outside, but the actual place where the Lord's idol is kept is very small. Inside the *garbha gṛha* it is always dark, and when you go near the altar, the priest will hold and offer a camphor-light by which you can see the form of the Lord.

What is the significance of all this? Subjectively, it means that the supreme Self, the Lord who is seated in my heart, is covered by the darkness of ignorance and is yet unknown and unseen by me. The camphor offered by the priest is nothing but solidified fragrance; when it is burnt up, nothing remains to be seen. This fragrance is called *vāsa* or *vāsanā* in Sanskrit and it represents all the negative tendencies and impressions in our minds. The solidified *vāsanās* in us, the ego, manifests in the form of desires, likes, and dislikes. The lighting of the camphor in the temple ritual represents the kindling of the fire of knowledge within us and the burning up of the ego. In the light of that Knowledge we then behold the *Paramātman*, the Lord in our hearts.

At the end of the ritual, when the camphor-flame is shown to everyone present, they put their hands over the flame and then touch their own eyes. This gesture signifies that we want to keep permanently before our eyes that light in which we saw the Lord. What is seen by the eyes goes into the heart. Consequently, when we look at the created world we have this new vision of the Lord everywhere. The famous first verse of *Īśāvāsya Upaniṣad* also gives us this instruction: *Īśāvāsyam idaṃ sarvam*—"All this, whatsoever moves in this universe, including the universe, itself moving, is indwelt, pervaded, enveloped, or clothed by the Lord."

There is also a significance as to why we put a donation into the plate as the camphor-flame is being passed around. It means that when we gain this greater vision of the world we will become generous. Do not be a miser at that time, like some people who search their pockets for a smaller bill or put a large bill on the plate but take back change! Just as the money given in the temple is for the welfare of the whole community, when we experience God's presence everywhere our wealth and possessions are shared with others.

At the very end of the ritual there is the distribution of the food that has been offered to the Lord (*prasāda*). To most of us, *prasāda* means something that is edible, and that is all! But the real meaning of *prasāda* is "purity, cheerfulness, bliss, joy, peace." This is our true gain upon tuning our minds with the Lord during the worship. The real *prasāda* is the feeling of peace we experience in our hearts while looking at the idol of the Lord after we have performed our daily worship (*pūjā*) with great love and devotion. But generally, if we perform *pūjā* at all, we finish in two or three minutes and say, "Done! Finished!" That is why the *prasāda*, the peace and joy, is not experienced by us—because we do not know how to tune our minds to the Lord.

So far I have explained the need for, and the significance of the temple and the rituals, which are vast sciences in themselves. But knowing even this much is a beautiful thing.

The Symbology of the Idol

In Hinduism the various forms of the Lord are for meditation. For each form there is an accompanying verse called a *dhyāna śloka*, which describes each aspect of that particular deity's form, according to which an artist sculpts or paints the picture. Though we are given this outer form to look at, we are to meditate on its subtler meaning.

Let us take an example of a famous *dhyāna śloka* associated with Lord Vishnu:

> *Śāntākāraṃ bhujagaśayanaṃ padmanābhaṃ sureśaṃ*
> *Viśvādhāraṃ gaganasadṛśaṃ meghavarṇaṃ śubhāṅgam*

Lakṣmīkāntaṃ kamalanayanaṃ yogibhir dhyānagamyaṃ
Vande viṣṇuṃ bhavabhayaharaṃ sarvalokaikanātham.

Vande viṣṇuṃ means I salute the Lord Vishnu. Etymologically *Viṣṇu* means "all-pervading." *Yogibhir dhyānagamyaṃ* means that the true nature of the Lord is experienced by yogis in meditation. With our eyes we may see an idol, but the reality of it, the essential nature of Lord Vishnu, is experienced only by those great yogis who have realized the Truth through the long and deep practice of meditation.

The first line of the verse explains the true nature of Vishnu. He is *śāntākāraṃ*—of the very nature of absolute peace. In that Reality there is no disturbance of any kind because the mind has not yet arisen with its thought-agitations and turbulence. Where there is no mind, there is absolute peace. Therefore, *śāntākāraṃ* refers to the Lord (the Self) abiding in His own absolute nature.

Bhujagaśayanaṃ means the one who is reclining on the snake. The snake is also called *Śeṣa* in Sanskrit, which means that which remains when everything else is gone. From one standpoint, *śeṣa* refers to time; when all things that are born disappear, time alone remains. Time swallows the whole world yet is itself still existent. In the *Bhāgavata Purāṇa*, it is said that the snake also represents the unmanifest *prakṛti*, the condition of the world before its manifest creation—when the forms and characteristics of all beings and things remain in a state of latency and non-differentiation. This state is compared to our deep-sleep state, in which, due to the absence of thought modifications, we no longer experience an individual identity or a separate pluralistic world.

This *bhujagaśayanaṃ* aspect of Lord Vishnu can represent, therefore, either the supreme Self existing as the cosmic time factor, or as the unmanifest condition of *prakṛti*, the world.

As you can see from these explanations, God-symbolism has a language of its own, for which we need to have the knowledge of Vedanta in order to properly understand it.

The next verse describes Lord Vishnu as *padmanābhaṃ*. In pictures portraying Lord Vishnu we see that a lotus is growing from his navel! What can this possibly mean? In Sanskrit, the word for lotus is *kamala*. *Ka* means "water, joy, *Brahman*"; *mala* means "dirt." One meaning of *kamala* is "the dirt of water." But here, dirt really refers to that which comes out from oneself. Perspiration comes out from our own body, and when it dries up, it becomes blackish dirt. This dirt is from our own self, not from anywhere else. So too, in this symbol, the lotus refers to that which is coming out of *Brahman*, the navel or center of all creation. And what is that? It is the very first thought-disturbance of "I-consciousness" arising from the supreme, infinite Consciousness.

When I am lying down in deep-sleep, I am in my own unmanifest nature (*avyakta*), in which there is no creation or world for me at all. When I wake up, the very first thought is the consciousness that "I am." Thereafter, my entire world of thoughts, feelings, and objects is created for me once again. That is why Lord Brahma, who is shown sitting inside the lotus, has four faces. If we think about it subjectively we find that for everything we create and in every action there are four stages. In other words, the mind, represented by Lord Brahma, has four aspects. First, a thought arises in the mind, "Why not go to this talk on Indian culture?" This stage is represented by the first mouth of Lord Brahma, which is called *saṅkalpa*. But just because the thought has arisen, it does not necessarily mean we will go. The second mouth reflects the stage of decision, *niścaya*; "Yes, I will go." But why have we decided this way? Because of the memory of a prior experience, as we think, "Last week I went to the talk and it was all right. Swamiji is not that bad. I guess I can do it for forty-five minutes." Due to a memory of the past we make a decision in the present. Memory, therefore, is represented by the third "mouth" in the process of creation and is called *smṛti*. Then, finally, we make a firm determination that we will definitely go to the talk and we get in our car and go! This final determination of the will is called *ahaṃkāra* (ego) and is reflected in the fourth mouth of Lord Brahma. Is it not true that every creation comes about in these four stages?

Thus, the sequence given so far is as follows: First, the pure Consciousness in its absolute nature is described as *śāntākāraṃ*; in association with the *avyakta avasthā*, the state or time of unmanifest *prakṛti*, the Lord is described as *bhujagaśayanaṃ* lying on the bed of snakes; then the lotus of "I-consciousness," along with the four aspects of the mind, arises from that pure Consciousness and begins the process of creation; here He is called *padmanābhaṃ*.

The last word in the first line of the *dhyāna śloka* is *sureśaṃ*, meaning Lord of the *Suras*, the gods. The lesser gods or *devas* of Hinduism represent the manifested forces of nature and also their presiding deities, such as Agni, god of fire, who is said to be the presiding deity of the organ and function of speech. Lord Vishnu, the pure Consciousness, is beyond all conditionings of nature—He is nature's very source and so also its lord and master.

The second line of the verse begins with *viśvādhāraṃ* (sometimes called *viśvākāraṃ*), meaning that Lord Vishnu, the pure Consciousness, is the very support of the universe, the substratum of the world, and this Consciousness is itself appearing as this universe.

Gaganasadṛśaṃ means "like all-pervading space." Just as space is all-pervading yet unseen, and though it gives accommodation to everything, it remains unpolluted, untouched (*nirmala*); the same is true of the pure Consciousness, which is *Brahman*.

Meghavarṇaṃ means "the [blue] color of a water-bearing cloud." Blue is the color of infinity. Just as the sky and the vast expanse of oceanic waters appear blue because the eyes cannot see their limits, so too, even though the Lord may take a particular incarnation as Rama or Krishna, His nature remains ever infinite.

Śubāṅgaṃ means "the one whose body (limbs) is auspicious and pure," because He is, by nature, absolute purity without any stain of ignorance.

Lakṣmīkāntaṃ means "the beloved Lord of Lakshmi." Lakshmi is none other than the Lord's own power of creation, *śakti*. Lakshmi never stays where Lord Vishnu is not. This indicates that the creative power, nature, or *prakṛti*, as we call it, cannot exist or function without the presence of Life, the pure Consciousness that illumines and enlivens it.

Kamalanayanaṃ is "the lotus-eyed one," whose eyes are cheerful, fully blossomed and beautiful, not sleepy like ours. The lotus, as I mentioned before, also indicates purity, for, due to its waxy coating, the petals remain untouched by the water in which they grow.

From the above descriptions, we can see what a profound verse this is on Lord Vishnu. Without this understanding, we normally chant the verse without appreciating its deeper implications.

In essence, the language of God-symbolism tells us that if we meditate on the various aspects of the Lord's form with correct understanding, we can realize the true essence of what is represented by that outer symbol. Through it we can know the nature of the absolute Reality beyond all names and forms and can understand the entire creation along with its various states. We also realize that even while all this creation is appearing in Consciousness, the Lord, the Self, still remains in His own infinite glory. This is true meditation.

If we do not have immediate understanding of the higher and subtler implications of the symbol, we can begin by worshiping the idol. Tuning our minds to it and developing love for it. Then, after some time, we will begin to ask, "What is it that I am worshiping?" Until this question arises in the mind, the practice of *pūjā* is incomplete and more thinking is required, but once it has, the worship is fruitful and its true purpose is fulfilled.

I have described the meaning of this one God-symbol according to its accompanying verse for meditation. For every Hindu deity there is a *dhyāna śloka,* which is to be meditated upon in this way. Once we know that such wonderful Truth is being depicted in the picture or idol and we worship and meditate on it with this understanding, it will be a beautiful experience.

VII

Installation of the Religious Idol

Rituals pertaining to the installation and consecration of the religious idol in the temple is another important topic about which we should know.

The ceremony in which the idol is installed in a particular place in the home, community center, or temple is called the *mūrti sthāpana*. When the idol is installed at home or in a community center, there are no strict rules regarding the method of worship; the idol's presence is mainly to aid us in our meditation. In regular temples, however, we not only perform the *mūrti sthāpana*, but also another consecration ceremony called the *prāṇa pratiṣṭhā*. *Prāṇa* means "life" and *pratiṣṭhā* means "placing." *Prāṇa pratiṣṭhā*, therefore, means "the placing or infusing of life into the idol." Thereafter the idol is no longer looked upon as merely an idol, but as a living entity.

Without breath, the human body is only a physical structure, and we need not care for it the way we do of a living entity that must be fed, clothed, bathed, rested, and so on. In the same way, when we buy a *mūrti* (idol or image of God) from the marketplace, it is just a physical form for which no elaborate rituals are necessary; but when the *prāṇa pratiṣṭhā* is performed, life is infused into the idol. Everyday thereafter, the deity must be bathed, offered food, clothes, and ornaments, along with other articles of worship such as incense, lights, and performance of the full *āratī*.

Whenever an opportunity arises, please observe a *prāṇa pratiṣṭhā* ceremony at a temple. Very few people really pay close attention during an ordinary *pūjā*. They say, "Oh, we do not understand anything the priest is doing or what he is chanting." But many do not even try to understand. We cannot blame only the priest class or others for our ignorance. We ourselves must be serious in learning the meaning of the ceremony. The ceremony comprises several steps each having its own significance.

Navagraha Pūjā

Ganeśa Pūjā and *Navagraha Pūjā* form the preliminary steps of the worship of the main diety to be consecrated. For this, many copper pots (*kalaśas*) are brought to the temple and filled with Ganga water. For two or three days, *pūjās* are performed and mantras are chanted, whereby the water is charged with spiritual force. This chanting of mantras is similar to the way batteries or wires are charged with electrical energy. A plain wire by itself is called a "dead" wire. It has no capacity to energize or electrify; but when an electric current is passed through it, it is called a "live" wire and can be used to empower various equipments. Though a good battery and a dead one may look the same, only the battery that is sufficiently charged will start the car engine.

Sound can have a great effect not only on water but on our bodies also, and that is why, even today, sound-therapy is employed. A case in point is that of a brahmin who performed various rituals for people and then was given sumptuous food by them. Although he was diabetic, he loved sweets and could not resist them. Fortunately, this brahmin knew the *Saura Sūkta*, a Vedic hymn to the sun, which he started to chant at home after he had eaten a lot of sweets. After chanting the mantra a certain number of times his body would sweat profusely. Afterwards, when he went to the doctor for a blood sugar test, it was found that he had no ill effects from the sugar whatsoever! It has even been proven that when one chants ancient Vedic mantras without understanding their meaning, positive effects are produced on the body. This is the power of the Vedic mantras!

In Hinduism, this science of sound is described in the *mantra śāstra*, which explains the different mantras that affect the particular parts of the body and mind. This power of sound also explains why we feel so peaceful when we go to temples where mantras are being chanted, for even though we cannot see the power, we feel it; and we say that there is a spiritual vibration.

In the same way, the water placed in the copper pots for the *Navagraha Pūjā* is charged with spiritual energy through Vedic mantras and worship. The idol is then taken to a special place for installation. The copper pots are carried on the heads of the priests or of a *sannyāsī* (renunciate) attending the ceremony, and the water is poured onto the idol. After this, the priest or *sannyāsī* "closes" the eyes of the idol by applying *candana* (sandalwood paste) and pressing his thumbs on the idol's eyes. The eyes are again "opened" when he removes his thumbs. The idol is then regarded as a living god and not just as a piece of stone or wood.

When the ceremony is performed properly and daily worship is offered by the priest, and more and more people come with faith to offer their prayers and prostrations, the idol gains power. Though this may sound strange it is something like an ordinary person becoming an officer and gaining more power and authority as increasing numbers of people come to him for help and decision-making. The more people look up to him, the more his power increases. In the same way, as more reverence is bestowed upon the idol, it, in turn, gains greater power to bless us.

Kumbhābhiṣeka

In the consecration ceremony, there is another aspect called the *kumbhābhiṣeka*. *Abhiṣeka*, in general, means "bathing" and is derived from the Sanskrit root *sic*, "to sprinkle," to which is prefixed *abhi*, "all around." For the *kumbhābhiṣeka*, a golden pot (*kalaśa*) is kept on the top of the temple. Consecrated water is then brought and poured into this pot.

What is the significance of having the idol inside the temple and a *kalaśa* above it? The idol—such as Ganesha, Shiva, or Vishnu—has a particular form; its presence in the temple represents the personal, *saguṇa* (with form) aspect of *Brahman*, the Reality. The *kalaśa* on top of the temple is not in the shape of any person, however, and so it represents the attributeless, *nirguṇa* (without form) aspect of Reality.

A person approaching the temple from a distance is able to see the *kalaśa* on top, but he or she enters the temple first to worship the personal form of the Lord inside. Subjectively, this means that from a distance we see the highest goal we want to attain—the formless, *nirguṇa Brahman*—but in order to reach there, we must go through the practice of worshiping the *saguṇa* aspect of the Lord. Thus the path for the spiritual aspirant is indicated. Through worship of the Lord (with attributes), we reach the highest, formless *Brahman*.

The Sixteen Steps of Pūjā

In the main *pūjā* of the temple deity there is a correct sequence of steps to be performed. For the removal of any obstacles and for the successful completion of the *pūjā*, one must begin with an invocation of Lord Ganesha, followed by prayers to Goddess Sarasvati and the guru. The *Kalaśa Pūjā*, or sanctification of the water is next, followed by the *Dravya Pūjā*, the consecration of the materials to be offered to the Lord. An *Ātmā Pūjā* is also done for the purification of one's own self. (At this time the priest puts a flower on his own head.)

After these initial procedures are done, the 16 steps of the *Ṣoḍaśa Upacāra Pūjā* begin. Many of these formalities are services we perform daily for our own bodies and for others. For instance, when a guest comes to our house, we welcome him, give him a place to sit, and an opportunity to take a bath, and then we offer him food and entertainment. When we bid him farewell, we do so only with the promise that he will visit again. In this *pūjā*, it is the Lord Himself whom we are welcoming as our guest. And this welcome, in the form of a prayer, is called *āvāhana*. The deity is offered a seat (*āsana*), water is offered for washing His feet and hands and for drinking.

After this, the deity is bathed (*snāna*). While being bathed,

Puruṣa Sūkta is chanted for Lord Vishnu or *Rudra Camaka* for Lord Shiva. Lord Shiva must be bathed continuously, therefore a *kalaśa* with a small hole is hung above the idol, and water drips out slowly upon it. This continuous stream of water represents the unbroken mental thought of the Lord, *sajātīya vṛtti pravāha*, and indicates that our contemplation on God should be continuous, effortless, and single-pointed. While watching this stream of water on the Shiva idol and while chanting the mantras, one's mind cannot help but become single-pointed. This will not happen if the water is poured out upon the idol suddenly, all at once.

After bathing, fresh clothes are offered to the deity along with the anointing by *candana* and *kum kum*. The deity is decorated with new ornaments and offered incense (*dhūpa*), a lamp (*dīpa*), and freshly cooked food (*naivedya*).

The last step is the *āratī*, during which camphor (*karpūra*) is lit before the deity, symbolizing the light by which one sees the Lord's form. When we put our hands over the flame and then touch our eyes, it means that we try to keep that light or vision of the Lord ever in front of our eyes and look upon the world from this new divine standpoint.

The food that has been offered to the Lord becomes *prasāda*, blessed food, and our partaking of this *prasāda* indicates *ānanda śānti*, the blissful peace that we experience upon realization of God.

Pūjās conducted outside the temple, conclude with a "farewell" prayer to the deity. This is not done in the temple *pūjā* because the temple is considered to be the Lord's permanent abode.

These are, in brief, the sixteen steps of the *Ṣoḍaśa Upacāra Pūjā*.

This *pūjā* can be done even in our own home. Though one may not go through all the steps elaborately, incense and lights can at least be offered. By doing this every day, we start communicating with the Lord.

When two persons sit and talk together, we do not wonder at it. Some people communicate with their pets and seem to know what the pets are saying by the way they wag their tail or bark. An outside observer may not understand anything, but a person who is in tune with the animal can certainly communicate. There are people, especially gardeners, who can communicate with trees and flowers. Going a step beyond this, people who worship a religious idol with great faith and devotion become so attuned to it that the idol actually "speaks" to them. If the devotee has a problem and sits in front of the idol, the answer to the question comes to his or her mind. Bharata, the brother of Bhagavan Ramachandra, used to worship the sandals (*pādukās*) of Sri Rama and it is said that whenever he had any doubts, he used to sit in front of the *pādukās* and they would talk to him.

Of course, we need not take the word "talking" in just the literal sense. What is meant is that when the mind becomes calm, quiet, and attuned with the beloved idol through faith and devotion, the answers come into the mind of the devotee.

There are some devotees who are so in tune with their idols that they use cool water to bathe the deity in the summer and have a fan for it also; and in the winter, they use hot water. On the other hand, there are some insensitive people who will use hot water to bathe themselves in winter but only cold water for the deity. This only shows that their hearts are very cold and the very purpose of the worship is left unfulfilled.

If *pūjā* is done regularly, sincerely, and with great devotion, we will find that our mind becomes purified and at one with the *mūrti* (idol). The practice of *pūjā* is a science in itself and is also a matter of faith and devotion. There are books that describe all these *pūjās* in great detail. However, the best thing is to observe one of these rituals, to take an interest in it, and to inquire into the meaning of what is being done. Thus we come to enjoy this practice.

VIII

Symbolism of Lord Shiva

Having explained the symbolism of Lord Vishnu, let us discuss the symbolism of Lord Shiva and His attributes. Before doing so, however, I will mention a few points concerning Lord Brahma, the Creator.

Many people ask why there are so many temples dedicated to Lord Vishnu, Shiva, the Divine Mother, Rama, Krishna, Ganesha, and other deities, but so few dedicated to Lord Brahma. In fact, the only famous temple for Lord Brahma in India is in Pushkar, in the state of Rajasthan. When I was traveling, however, I discovered that the greatest worship devoted to Lord Brahma is in Bangkok, Thailand. Aside from the many small temples dedicated to him, there is a very large and famous temple that has become a tourist attraction. I asked why there are so many temples for Lord Brahma in Thailand even though it is primarily a Buddhist country and I received an interesting explanation.

Before this large temple was built, there was another building under construction in that same area, where many workers were having fatal accidents. The people wondered what they should do and decided to worship Lord Brahma since He is the god of creation. After they worshiped Lord Brahma, it is said that there were no more accidents and the building was successfully completed. Thereafter, His worship became very popular. This is only one explanation I have heard concerning the worship of Lord Brahma in Thailand, though there may be others as well.

As to why there are so few temples dedicated to Lord Brahma in India, Swami Chinmayananda once explained it in the following way: He said that our minds continuously and effortlessly entertain thoughts of doing and creating. We have no difficulty creating thoughts in our minds; the only problem is that we do not know how to sustain and destroy those thoughts very well! For instance, the thoughts "let me buy a car" or "let me buy a house" arise very easily, but often we do not have the power to maintain that thought long enough to achieve the goal. We do not know how to sustain a noble thought in our minds when it arises, nor, on the other hand, do we know how to destroy ignoble thoughts. In other words, creating thoughts is spontaneous and natural to us, but the other two faculties of maintenance and destruction are much more difficult.

In addition our thought-creations become difficult to get rid of when necessary. Having created so many attachments and entanglements in our lives, we become helpless and cannot free ourselves from them. Therefore, we need the inner power of destruction. This is why we invoke Lord Shiva—to give us the capacity to destroy all our attachments and unwanted thoughts. We also need the grace and blessings of Lord Vishnu to sustain our noble thoughts and to make them consistent until we reach our goal. This is the reason that we need more temples dedicated to Lord Vishnu and Lord Shiva, but for Lord Brahma one is quite enough!

The Many Facets of Lord Shiva

As observed previously, every god and goddess in Hinduism can be understood from at least four different standpoints: the absolute, the cosmic, the "departmental" (in charge of a particular aspect of creation), and the incarnation who appeared on earth to reestablish *dharma*.

From the highest standpoint, Lord Shiva is the formless, absolute Reality, which is of the nature of pure Consciousness. Shiva's name itself means auspiciousness. Interestingly, there is a similar-sounding word in Sanskrit, *śava*, which means a dead body. A body itself is nothing but inert matter—a corpse; but in the living form, Shiva's presence transforms the body into a beautiful and holy thing, because of which we bestow love, honor, or affection upon a person. That divine Presence is the pure Consciousness, Shiva, auspiciousness, and it is our own true nature.

From the cosmic standpoint, Lord Shiva represents the Lord of the Universe—the creator, sustainer, and destroyer of the world. From the departmental standpoint Lord Shiva is worshiped as the deity in charge of the power of destruction, while Lord Brahma is considered to be the creator and Lord Vishnu, the deity in charge of sustenance. However, since there can be no creation without destruction nor any destruction without creation, we cannot attribute the power of creation exclusively to one deity and the power of destruction to another. Our distinction between these three powers is merely to help clarify the various processes of life.

In His fourth aspect, as a particular form that manifested on earth, Lord Shiva is said to have appeared in numerous incarnations as a *guru avatāra*, an enlightened Master who teaches the knowledge of the Self to his disciples. Sri Adi Shankaracharya and Dakshinamurti Bhagavan were considered to be such *avatāras* of Lord Shiva.

In his *Rāmāyaṇa*, Goswami Tulsidas explains that Lord Shiva is *Brahman*, the absolute Reality, and Parvati, his spouse, is *Ādi-Śakti*, the Lord's primordial power. Saint Tulsidas also gives another dimension of Lord Shiva and says:

> I salute Bhavani (Parvati) and Shankara (Shiva) who are the embodiments of faith, without whom even great seekers cannot realize the highest Reality in their hearts.

Lord Shiva, therefore, is not only the supreme Reality present in every heart, but He is also the faith that is essential to realize the Truth. Yet even if we have faith, we are not able to see the Truth unless we have a teacher to guide us. Therefore, Saint Tulsidas says further, "I salute the Guru, Shankara, who is the embodiment of eternal Knowledge." In the Hindu scriptures, Lord Shiva is the supreme *Brahman*, the faith by which we realize that Truth, and also the guru who guides us.

Tulsidas gives another beautiful verse on Lord Shiva in the *Rāmacaritamānasa,* which is full of deep significance:

> yasyāṇke ca vibhāti bhūdharasutā devāpagā mastake
> bhāle bālavidhur gale ca garalaṃ yasyorasi vyālarāṭ
> so'yaṃ bhūtivibhūṣaṇaḥ suravaraḥ sarvādhipaḥ sarvadā
> śarvaḥ sarvagataḥ śivaḥ śaśinibhaḥ śrīśaṅkaraḥ pātu mām.

Śrī Śaṅkaraḥ pātu mām—May that Lord Shankara protect me. Shankara, another name for Lord Shiva, is derived from *śama*-auspiciousness—and *kara*—He who brings. Lord Shiva is the one who brings auspiciousness into our lives.

Yasyāṅke ca vibhāti bhūdharasutā. In the first line of this verse, Saint Tulsidas salutes Lord Shiva as He on whose left side sits the beautiful goddess Parvati and on whose head is the goddess Ganga (*devāpagā mastake*). Even though there are beautiful goddesses above and beside him, Lord Shiva is never distracted and is ever in meditation! In our cases, as we know if we have practiced meditation, the slightest scent of perfume distracts our attention! This picture of Lord Shiva with the two goddesses shows us His power of concentration and meditation.

The River Gaṅgā

The river Ganga on Lord Shiva's head has several interpretations. By some it is said that she is *Jñāna Gaṅgā*, the flow of knowledge from teacher to disciple, as we conceive of knowledge flowing into the head. Saint Tulsidas gives another interpretation: He says that Ganga represents devotion to Lord Rama. Whether we say devotion or knowledge, both are the same, for just as we keep knowledge in the head, we must also revere and sustain the attitude of devotion in our minds.

When someone asked me why Lord Shiva had Ganga on His head I told him, "He is showing you that you should keep your head cool!" This meaning is also important because, in general, we are very hot-headed people! There is a saying in Hindi that the sign of a healthy person is one whose feet are warm, whose stomach is soft, and whose head is cool! For most of us, it is just the opposite; we get "cold feet" (a sense of isolation, fear, or reluctance toward life), our stomach gets upset from eating the wrong kind of food, and our head is hot with anger! I often tell people, "You have so many hangers in your house, why don't you hang your anger in the closet?" Just as we are able to take out our clothes and hang them up again, we should be able to remove or put away our anger when it arises. Keep the head cool and you win the world. A person who has no control over his temper becomes "temperamental"—fifty percent temper and fifty percent mental!

We can keep the head cool only through knowledge and devotion, just as Bharata did—to demonstrate his great love and respect for Sri Ramachandra—when he took the sandals of Sri Rama at Chitrakuta and kept them on his head as he went all the way back to Ayodhya.

The Crescent Moon

Bhāle bālavidhur gale ca garalaṃ: On Shiva's forehead is the crescent moon and in His neck is poison. The crescent moon that is seen on Lord Shiva's forehead represents the nectar of life. It is said that the nectarine rays of the moon fall on earth and nourish the entire vegetable kingdom. But poison is just the opposite—it brings death! Lord Shiva holds both the moon and the poison, yet is ever in meditation. This image has a deep significance, for it indicates that our lives are full of pairs of opposites: life and death, creation and destruction, joy and sorrow, honor and dishonor, success and failure. We should be able to bear these pairs of opposites with calmness of mind and not let them destroy our mental equipoise. Generally we want only life; we do not know how to handle death. We want only joy but not its opposite. The symbols of the crescent moon and the poison in Lord Shiva's neck indicate that we should be able to accept pain as well as pleasure and that we should have inner balance and equipoise in the midst of all good and bad experiences.

There is another meaning behind the moon on Lord Shiva's head. A crescent moon is not straight, it is curved and tilted. Saint Tulsidas explains that even though the moon is a little crooked, we overlook it while worshiping Lord Shiva. We do not tell the moon to get out of the way first and then worship the Lord! No. Because the moon is in association with the Lord, it is worshiped along with Him. This means that even though some disciples of the guru may be crooked or imperfect, they are given respect just because of their association with the guru. Though the disciple may never be invited anywhere by himself, if the guru is invited by someone, the disciple is asked to come along, so he also receives the glory!

The Blue-Necked One

One story in the Puranas explains how Lord Shiva came to have poison in his neck. In ages past, when the milky ocean was being churned by the gods and demons in order to get the nectar of immortality, the celestial snake, Vasuki, who was being used as the churning rope, began to vomit a fatal poison called *halāhala viṣa*. Until then, since many attractive and good things had been churned out of the ocean, the gods and demons had argued and fought over them; but when the poison came out of Vasuki, none of them wanted it. In desperation, they went to Lord Shiva and said, "O Lord, please save us from this poison which is burning the whole world even by its smell! No one else has as much power as you!" Because Lord Shiva is the embodiment of compassion (*karuṇā avatāra*), He took the poison and drank it. However, He did not swallow the poison entirely, but kept it in His throat without letting it go to His stomach. The poison turned His neck blue, and that is how He came to be called the blue-necked One (*nīlakanṭha*).

The meaning behind this story is that only a great and wise person will be able to swallow all the poison in life. Ordinary people lay claim only to the good things in life—beauty, comfort, success, and so on, and even take credit for achieving them; but when they have bitter experiences, they reject them! Many ask, "Why is it that only good people suffer?" It is because only the good and noble ones have the capacity to suffer, whereas other people will break down under the same circumstances.

The fact that Lord Shiva did not swallow the poison entirely but kept it in His neck is significant: He did not become poisonous or bitter himself. Many people become very bitter themselves and then vomit it upon others. Lord Shiva neither swallowed the poison completely nor did he spit it out. Rather, as He held it in His neck, the poison beautified Him and became like an ornament. In the same way, one who is able to go through all experiences of life and still abide in his own true nature, without becoming bitter, becomes another Lord Shiva.

The Lord Himself has said that if a person is capable of enduring suffering and of removing the suffering of another, that person should do so. If he does not do this he will incur sin. However, one should not grumble and complain while suffering, instead the mind should always be immersed in inner meditation.

The Snake Garland

Yasyorasi vyālarāṭ—He is adorned with the snake garland. People often ask why there is a snake around Lord Shiva's neck because, for most of us, the very mention of the word "snake" creates fear. This image of Lord Shiva shows us that He is fearless.

The snake also represents time (*kāla*). When a poisonous snake bites a victim the person dies. So too, the snake of time eventually catches up with and bites every created being. Time and death are ordinarily frightening ideas to us, but Lord Shiva is the Lord of time, indicating that the timeless Reality is our own nature too. How then can time and death frighten us?

The snake on Lord Shiva's neck can also represent the mind that spits out its poison of negative thoughts. Yet if we keep the mind under perfect control so that it is quiet within and no longer agitating ourselves or others, it will lie as peacefully in meditation as Lord Shiva Himself, neither hissing nor spitting.

So'yaṃ bhūtivibhūṣaṇaḥ—(Lord Shiva wears) ashes of the cremation ground smeared all over His body. These ashes are *vibhūti*, a great glory for Him. By this Lord Shiva shows us that our bodies are already dead, inert matter, which will turn to ashes one day. We should, therefore, rise above our identification with the body even while we are living.

The Ruler of All

Suravaraḥ sarvādhipaḥ sarvadā—(Lord Shiva is) the best among gods and is the ruler of the entire world. When one rises above one's body-identification does one not become a master of the world? Thereafter, can anyone frighten, tempt, bribe, or compel him to do anything wrong? No, for all our wrong actions, temptations, fears, insecurities, and corruptions arise only out of identification with the body. As long as this identification remains one can never become a master of situations. But Lord Shiva is the one who is able to destroy all these negativities; such a person becomes all-pervading and is famous everywhere (*sarvagataḥ*).

Śaśinibhaḥ means "He whose glow is like that of the moon, [which pleases everybody's heart]." This in turn makes the mind calm and quiet. Saint Tulsidas concludes by saying, "May that Lord Shiva protect me." Such is the beautiful representation of Lord Shiva's form in this verse. I have explained only a portion of its entire meaning.

The Three-Eyed One

Lord Shiva as *trilocana*, the three-eyed One, is another important aspect. It is said that the third eye, located between the eyebrows, is the eye of wisdom. The other two eyes represent love and justice. When the Lord looks at and deals with this world, He is both loving and just. Some people want to be just without compassion; but, in that case, justice becomes too harsh. On the other hand, if one is too loving, with no sense of justice, he becomes sentimental. This creates a problem because then the number of unjust, criminal people in society grows. Lord Shiva exemplifies a good ruler who has both love and justice and also looks at this world with the vision of Knowledge that destroys all ignorance and passion.

Thus we find that Lord Shiva represents the absolute Reality, the substratum of the world, and also the Self of all beings; He is the Master of the universe as well as the deity in charge of the total destruction of this world—the destruction that will subsequently bring about a new creation. In addition, Lord Shiva represents different incarnations of the guru, such as Sri Shankaracharya and Sri Dakshinamurti; and finally, He is the faith whereby we reach the Truth.

Please think more about these different aspects of Lord Shiva and, after gathering a greater understanding of Him, contemplate on the deeper meaning of His form.

IX

The Śāstras

The Vedas are said to be eternal. People question when they hear this: "What are you trying to tell us? How can the Vedas be eternal?" This confusion arises when we think of the Vedas merely as books. Certainly a book cannot be eternal. Yet, as has been mentioned before, the Vedas are actually a body of Knowledge, and Knowledge is not something which is produced; it is ever-existent—just as Newton's law of gravity is named after Newton, the scientist who discovered it, but did not create it. That law or force was ever-present in the universe; and the knowledge of it, therefore, was an ever-present possibility. This is why we never say that a scientific law has been created—only that it has been discovered—because the knowledge of it was covered at first by ignorance and then that cover was removed.

Once, in a chemistry class, the teacher told his students that oxygen was discovered in the sixteenth century, so one student asked, "What were people breathing before that time?" Did the teacher's statement mean that oxygen was not there prior to its discovery? Of course not. In the same way, Knowledge is eternal and the Vedas, which are synonymous with Knowledge, are also eternal.

Revelation

The Vedas are technically termed *śruti*, revealed knowledge. That they are revealed is an important point. They are not the composition of a human being, arrived at through intellectual and logical reasoning, based on sense perception. The Sanskrit verbal root *śru* means "to hear" and *śruti* means "that which is heard." When I hear something, that which is heard by me is not my own composition but is something spoken of or revealed by someone other than myself. For this reason, the Vedas are said to be *apauruṣeya*—not of human origin—and are considered as revelations.

But who revealed that Knowledge? The scriptures say: "The Vedas are the breath of God." Just as our breath emanates naturally and effortlessly from us as long as we are alive, the Vedas are considered to be the very breath of the Lord Himself. This Knowledge or Veda was effortlessly revealed by the Lord to those great rishis who had purified, tuned, and made their minds single-pointed through meditation. This reception of Knowledge is something like a radio, which, when tuned properly to the frequency of a particular radio station, receives the sound waves in the atmosphere and then reproduces the broadcasted program. When we hear the program we do not give credit to the radio by saying, "Oh, what a nice talk that radio gave!" In the same way, these pure-minded rishis were like receivers who had tuned their minds to the frequency or vibrations of the revelations of the Lord. Thus they were able to receive divine Knowledge, which they then imparted to their disciples. The rishis took no personal credit for what they heard and taught because that Knowledge was something ever-present and available to be known. If we can just learn to tune our minds to the Higher, we can all become great rishis. In summary, *śruti* is the "breath" of the Lord—eternal, revealed Knowledge.

The second category of scriptures is called *smṛti*. The Sanskrit root *smṛ* means "to remember" and *smṛti* means memory. Thus *smṛti śāstra* is knowledge that is remembered.

When we learn something from someone, and then teach it to others, our method of teaching will differ from person to person. Though all of us as students may learn from one and the same teacher, our individual ways of practicing and teaching that knowledge will be modified according to the time, need, circumstance, and the people to whom we are speaking. That knowledge which we teach and speak of from memory is called *smṛti*; we have not produced or created that knowledge, but are imparting it as we remember it.

Practical Application of Śruti

In the Vedic times there were great kings and rishis who had studied the Vedas and who had practiced, mastered, and experienced the essence of that Knowledge in their lives. There were other people, however, such as renunciates or householders, who approached them and said: "Sir, the Knowledge imparted by the *śruti* is very difficult for us to understand. Please teach us a more practical application of that Knowledge, which we can follow."

So this became the duty of the great masters—to communicate and teach the *śruti* according to the needs of the society at a particular time and place. This is always necessary, for times constantly change: Society is not static but dynamic. Although values are eternal, the way in which they are translated into action and lived in our lives varies.

In fact, it is all due to *smṛti śāstra* that the Hindu religion has survived through time, despite numerous invasions and onslaughts upon the culture. The great masters come from time to time to tell us not to become so rigid in our rituals, to be more flexible, and to live this Knowledge in a way that is suitable to the times. For instance, it is said that one should get up early, have a bath in the Ganga River, and offer prayers to Lord Sun. But how are we to do this nowadays? If we are not near the Ganga, we can go to any river in our vicinity. If there is no river in our town or if we live in a country other than India, it does not matter; we can just remember the Ganga while standing under the shower, wherever we are, and this itself will be *Gaṅgā snāna*. This is an example of a practical application of a *śruti* injunction, which, when taught by a master is called *smṛti*.

The second purpose of *smṛti śāstra* is to tell us what our specific duties and responsibilities are. When we are told by *śruti* to strictly perform our duties, dedicating them to the Lord, we always have the problem of knowing exactly what our duty is. Therefore, whether one is a student, householder, king, administrator, engineer, doctor, or lawyer, it is in the *smṛti śāstra* that we will find our specific duties pointed out.

Manu and Manu Smṛti

Many teachers, called *smṛti kāras*, have appeared in our society. As a result, we have many *smṛti śāstras,* such as *Parāśara Smṛti*, *Gautama Smṛti*, and *Kauṭilya Smṛti*. Even the *Bhagavad Gītā* is technically considered a *smṛti* because Lord Krishna remembered the Knowledge that was the essence of the Upanishads, and taught it to Arjuna in His own words. However, the *Gītā* has enjoyed the status of *śruti* due to the fact that it focuses more on spiritual knowledge than it does on day-to-day duties and observances.

For the understanding of our specific duties and for the benefit of society, the most famous and important *smṛti* is the *Manu smṛti*. As the name implies, this scripture originated with Manu, who was the mind-born son of the Creator, Lord Brahma. From the name Manu we get the Sanskrit words *manuṣya* and *mānava*, meaning human being; and later became "man" in English. Thus, in Hinduism, we are all regarded as the children of Manu.

When Lord Brahma started creating, it is said that Manu, the man, was born from one half of His mind and Shatarupa, a woman, was born from the other half. Shatarupa became Manu's wife and from these two came the rest of creation. We read a similar account in the Bible where God created Adam, and from Adam's rib Eve was created. Thereafter, they became the parents of all other human beings.

Manu's role in the universe was similar to that of a religious defense minister of the total cosmos—to protect *dharma* and see that people follow the righteous way of living. Manu assured the maintenance of *dharma* through prophets, devotees, and saints who come into the world from time to time.

Lord Brahma himself taught the *dharma śāstra* to Manu and it was Manu's duty to impart this Knowledge to the rishis, who, in turn, taught the rest of society. In the first chapter of the *Manu Smṛti*, therefore, we find Manu seated, while other rishis approach and prostrate to him, saying, "O great Lord, you know the mystery (*rahasya*), the essence of the *dharma śāstra*. Please teach it to us for the welfare of the entire society, for all people should know what is their common and specific *dharma*."

Manu answers by describing how the whole creation came forth from the one God. He tells them further that it was Lord Brahma who taught all this to him and that he has, in turn, taught Sage Bhrigu. Manu then requests Bhrigu to impart the Knowledge to the sages present. Thus the whole *Manu Smṛti* is made up of Rishi Bhrigu's discourses to all the other rishis.

The Problem of Desires

In the world we find that everyone engages in various activities to fulfill their desires. As *Manu Smṛti* says, "Whatever is done by a human being is prompted by some desire." Everyone believes that they will become happy when their desires are fulfilled; but this is the problem. In the process of trying to fulfill a desire, a strange thing happens, as *Manu Smṛti* explains in another verse: "Desires are not satiated by their fulfillment; the more one tries to satisfy them, the more they grow."

Curiously, we do not recognize that our attempts to fulfill a desire give rise to more desires, and hence they multiply. Though one may gain a temporary satisfaction, trying to quench a desire by fulfilling it is like trying to put out a fire by adding fuel to it—the fire only increases!

We also know that the more desires a person has, the more agitated his or her mind will be. As long as desire exists in the mind there will also be restlessness, fear, anxiety, and constant worry. "I do not know whether my desire will be fulfilled or not! How or when will it be fulfilled? If it is fulfilled how long will I be able to enjoy it?" As a consequence of these worries, many other negative emotions, such as anger and frustration arise. In other words, to be filled with desire is not a very desirable state!

The best principle, therefore, is to give up all desires. As the scriptures say, "Freedom from desire is total happiness."

At the same time to immediately become desireless is impossible.

We seem to be caught. So what should we do? Realizing that desires create problems and that desirelessness is good but seemingly impossible, can we live with these desires and fulfill them without creating new ones? At the same time, how can we grow out of our present desires? The beauty of the *dharma śāstra* is that it prescribes how to attain these goals, to rise above the desires and reach immortality. Dealing with this problem is the heart of and the art of the *dharma śāstra*.

Why is it essential to know this art? Let us take an analogy: We may try to avoid driving on the freeway as there is always a possibility of an accident. But if it is a necessity, then we should definitely learn the art of driving properly and know the laws of traffic so that we can reach our destination safely. Or we might feel it would be nice if we never had to eat. But we must eat in order to live. Yet once we start eating there is the other problem of not being able to stop, particularly when there is a lot of junk food or fast-food around! We may also develop a craving for one particular kind of food. But if we must eat, then we should certainly learn when to eat, how to eat, what to eat, and so on.

In the same way, our *smṛti kāras*, or teachers of *smṛti*, understood our problem. Though desirelessness is true happiness, a human being cannot suddenly become desireless. The scriptures help, therefore, by teaching us how to live and deal with our present desires without becoming slaves to them and how to ultimately grow out of these desires.

In conclusion then, the *smṛti śāstra* tells us that the best state to attain is "desirelessness," for the mind will then be ever at peace. Yet this state is not easily attained. We find it impossible to give up all our desires and to find permanent happiness by trying to fulfill them. This is our problem and to solve it we must have proper discrimination. Which desires should be fulfilled and in what manner? How can we live so that there is neither continuous restlessness of the mind nor suppression of it? The *dharma śāstra* teaches us how to live a life of discretion, of righteousness, and how to act and fulfill our desires in a way that will ultimately help us grow out of them. This will be the topic of our next chapter.

PART THREE

The Essence of Dharma

All weaknesses are transmuted into strengths
when the right spiritual values are accepted
and the seeker takes the daring resolve
to live the spiritual quest.

Swami Chinmayananda

Live your life, continuously, all the twenty-four hours, in the consciousness of the Divine and the Supreme, the True and the Eternal. Play the game of life: Play the part to which you have been called on the stage, but do not forget the greater mission in life, the greater goal that is to be achieved.

Live the stage-life perfectly, and play the part exactly as the Lord, the Manager and the Playwright, has intended it to be played. His intentions are codified and indicated in the great text books on *dharma*, which preach the higher values of life, that is, the ethical and moral rules of life. Live well. Live in kindness, love, and understanding.

Swami Chinmayananda

X

Indicators of Dharma

Exactly what is dharma? In the Vedas it is said: Four things determine what is *dharma*: *śruti*, *smṛti*, good noble conduct as accepted by society (*sadācāra*), and one's own joy and pleasure (*svasya ca priyam ātmanaḥ*). In other words, when we are performing an action, we can tell if it is our *dharma* by questioning whether or not the action is approved by *śruti* and *smṛti* (society's code of ethics) and by determining if the action gives us joy.

To understand how *dharma* is determined by *śruti* and *smṛti* we can compare how, in the United States, an action is considered legal or illegal according to the constitution laid down by the government. An action which is legal in this country may be illegal in another country, where the laws are different (as in the case of alcohol, which is legal in the United States, but prohibited in Arabian countries). Legality and illegality cannot be judged by the action itself, but by the constitution of that particular country. In the same way, only by knowing *śruti* and *smṛti* can we determine which actions are *dharmic*.

Although an action may be legal, it is not always considered moral. Or an action may be both legal and moral, but does not bring us happiness. We should understand, then, that if an action lacks one of these indications it is still not perfect *dharma*, for our actions should be in accordance with all four, which we call the *caturveda dharma lakṣaṇa*.

Religions often give injunctions, such as the Ten Commandments, that if you do one particular action it will be *adharmic* (unrighteous), and if you do another, it will be *dharmic*. However, this gives only a very general outline of *dharma*, for there are many difficult and complicated situations in life for which there are no easy, black-and-white solutions.

The *śruti* and *smṛti* also provide a general understanding of *dharma* and *adharma*, which most of us have heard from childhood: "Speak the truth, speak pleasingly, speak for the welfare of others (briefly), and speak as a friend." The scriptures also say, "do not eat meat" and "do not take alcohol." These actions are *adharmic*, and we see clearly what results from indulgence in them. For instance, the influence of alcohol prevents the mind from functioning properly and makes accident statistics soar!

The First Aspect

Smṛti śāstra tells us *ācāraḥ prathamo dharmaḥ*. "In following *dharma*, the first and foremost aspect is good conduct in life." *Ācāra* is the ability to discriminate whether our actions are in accordance with the moral values of the society in which we live. The scriptures clearly say that a person may be learned and scholarly, a knower of the Vedas, an expert in conducting rituals or in giving religious discourses, but if his conduct is not virtuous, then all his erudition is useless. On the other hand, a person with little scholarship and learning, but whose conduct is good, will be much more respected by others.

Ravana, for instance, was a great devotee of Lord Shiva, who, while performing rituals, used to cut off one of his heads (he had ten) to offer it to the Lord. For this sacrifice, Lord Shiva gave Ravana the boon of having a new head grow back each time one was cut off in battle. Even though Ravana made such a personal sacrifice, can we consider him a great devotee? No, because his conduct in life in other ways was not good at all. Others, like Hiranyakashipu, whom we read about in the scriptures, were also men of great rituals and penance, but with no love, compassion, or sympathy for people in their hearts; they were considered to be only *rākṣasas* (demons).

It is interesting to note that when you read the Sanskrit word *rākṣasa* backwards, from right to left, it becomes *sākṣara*. *Akṣara*, in general, refers to the alphabet and literature, and *sākṣara* means one who knows the alphabet, who is an educated, literate person. So ironically it is said, "When literate people (*sākṣaras*) become perverted in their minds they become *rākṣasas*." These are not beings with horns and tails, but the educated, literate people who have become crooked and perverted. For instance, many politicians think that their private lives and actions are above all laws and moral codes. But the truth is that as long as we are a part of society, especially if we are leaders and in the public eye, there is no such thing as being beyond the law—even in our private life we are held accountable for everything we do.

Duty Before Questions

Another important meaning of *ācāraḥ prathamo dharmaḥ* is that we should learn to obey and do our duty first, before asking a lot of questions. When it comes to doing our duties, however, first we generally ask, "Why?" To ask why is very easy, but we do not always have the maturity or knowledge to understand the entire principle and foundation of *dharma*.

At this moment we all have our likes and dislikes; we get carried away by them and do only what we like, not what we do not like. Consequently, our discrimination becomes clouded and when difficult situations arise in life, we do not know how to make decisions and act correctly. This is because we have never practiced living according to *dharma*, but have lived only according to our own whims and fancies. When we learn to listen and obey the scriptures first, however, the mind gradually becomes purer and we then understand the whole principle of *dharma*.

The two important meanings of the scriptural injunction *ācārah prathamo dharmaḥ* (good conduct comes first) are: that one should do one's duty before asking many questions; and secondly, in spiritual life good behavior is of foremost importance. We may have performed many rituals, built many temples, or given many discourses on Vedanta, yet if our conduct remains poor these actions are all meaningless.

Actions That Give Joy

The fourth indication of *dharma*, whether an action gives joy, is also very important. If an action causes agitations or guilt and we say, "Why did I do that?" then that action is not completely *dharmic*—even though it may be approved on all other counts (by *śruti*, *smṛti*, and *sadācāra*).

At the same time, though I may like or enjoy something, the question is, what is its effect on my life and mind? A person may say, "I feel very happy when I drink," but if *śruti* and *smṛti* do not approve of it, then it is not a *dharmic* action.

A still deeper implication of *svasya ca priyam ātmanaḥ* is as follows: We care for our happiness and do not want sorrow in our lives, and we should respect the fact that others also want happiness in their lives. Therefore, we have no right to cause other people unhappiness in the process of gaining happiness for ourselves. To destroy, harm, or hurt other people is *adharmic*.

Although determination of *dharma* is not always very easy, it can become simple if we have a sincere desire to live a good, *dharmic* life and are completely honest with ourselves. Then everything will fall into place naturally.

Two Types of Dharma

Essentially, there are two kinds of dharma pointed out in the scriptures: one that we call *sanātana dharma*, the eternal, universal values to be followed by all people in life, irrespective of nationality, age, profession, or station; and the second, called *varṇāśrama dharma*, the specific duties given to each individual with respect to his or her age, sex, status in society, and so on.

The Sanskrit word *dharma* means that which holds everyone and everything together—that which integrates the personality and unifies the society. We know that what *śruti* and *smṛti* point out as good conduct and as one's own joy is *dharmic*, because if we follow those actions, they will lead to an integrated personality within and thereby an integrated society without. *Dharma* is also defined as: that which leads you to material prosperity here in this world, and spiritual realization in this very life. *Dharma* is that which gives us both material prosperity and spiritual unfoldment.

Sanātana Dharma

Manu Bhagavan has said: "There are ten values in life that characterize *dharma* and that should be followed by all people." These ten values are: *dhṛti* (fortitude or forbearance), *kṣamā* (forgiveness or the ability to endure cheerfully), *dama* (control over our organs of action), *asteya* (non-stealing), *śauca* (purity), *indriya-nigraha* (mastery over the organs of perception), *dhī* (using the faculty of discrimination), *vidyā* (knowledge), *satya* (truthfulness), and *akrodha* (absence of anger). Are these values not necessary for all people at all times? It is for this reason that they are called *sanātana*, eternal and universal.

(1) Fortitude: *Dhṛti* means the capacity to hold onto something. In the eighteenth chapter of the *Bhagavad Gītā*, *dhṛti* is said to be of three kinds: *tāmasic*, *rājasic*, and *sāttvic*. *Tāmasic dhṛti* is holding onto things such as sleep, food, and wrong notions. *Rājasic dhṛti* is holding onto money, power, and pleasure, for which we are ready to do anything. *Sāttvic dhṛti* is the ability to rise above all obstacles, difficulties, and doubts while pursuing a noble goal in life. A person with such *dhṛti* may be physically or mentally tired or may even question why he is doing certain work, but he will remind himself again and again, "No, I must hold onto this goal." Whenever we mention *dhṛti* from now on, we will be referring to this *sāttvic dhṛti*—that strength, force, or ability with which we hold onto our noble values of life.

(2) Forgiveness: *Kṣamā* is forgiveness. The highest form of forgiveness is when the feeling of being offended does not even arise in the first place. Once a lady felt very offended by something that her husband had done, and her husband begged her to please forgive him. She finally did. Yet once in a while the wife would again remind her husband that she had forgiven him. Exasperated, the man finally asked, "You said long ago you had forgiven me, so why do you keep reminding me of it?" His wife said, "Well, I just do not want you to forget that I have forgiven

you!" Can this be an example of real forgiveness? No, for the greatest form of *kṣamā* is to never have felt any initial offense, insult, or hurt.

(3) Control of the sense organs: *Dama* means the control over our organs of action. If we get angry at someone and immediately want to strike out at him, this is not *dama*. However, if we are not able to control the feeling of anger rising in our mind, but are at least able to control the outward expression of it, this shows some degree of *dama*. Without even this much control, we only act on impulse and become worse than an animal.

(4) Non-stealing: *Asteya* means not taking another's possessions. What right do we have to deprive someone of their wealth, prosperity, or achievement?

There was a thief who used to steal from various houses and bring the stolen objects home with him. Then one day another thief broke into the first thief's house and took away everything. The first thief became very upset and his wife said to him, "Why are you crying now? You took all those things away from other people and started calling them your own. You never earned or produced any wealth yourself, yet you are crying as if the things were yours. Just think how those people from whom you stole must have cried!"

When a person has worked hard, he has earned his belongings. If we want to have those objects also, we must work hard to get them. Do not say we worked hard to enter someone else's house to steal his things! That is not called hard work; it is called criminal activity. *Asteya* means that even the thought of taking someone else's wealth should not arise in the mind!

(5) Purity: What is purity (*śauca*)? Purity does not mean standing under the shower for an hour with all the possible shampoos and soaps that are available in the market—soaps for the face, hands, back, for before bath, during bath, and after bath! Yes, physical cleanliness is also a part of purity, but the most important is our purity of motive. Outwardly our action may look very noble, but inwardly our attitude may not be all that good. Therefore, for every action we perform, each of us must be aware of whether or not our intentions are pure.

(6) Control over the Organs of Perception: Control over the sense organs determines what we should see, hear, taste, touch, and so on. This control is very important and requires discrimination. If we know that by seeing or hearing certain things our mind will be polluted or agitated with desire, we should not allow ourselves to see or hear them.

(7) Discrimination: The word *dhī* is the intellect, or faculty of discrimination, and means the ability to control oneself. It is only with this discriminative faculty that we can practice *dama* or adhere to *dharma* at all.

(8) Knowledge: One must also know what is true Knowledge, *vidyā*. Is knowledge merely the ability to read and write in order to get a job and earn a livelihood? The scriptures say, "The Knowledge that liberates one from all psychological entanglements is the only real Knowledge," and that is the knowledge of the Self. No doubt, we must have a job and earn money in order to live in the world, but we must also know the real, final goal of all our learning and effort.

(9) Truthfulness: *Satya* means truthfulness. When we make a promise, we should fulfill it. Whatever we speak should be true; and what is true, that alone we should speak. Always verify the truth of a statement before saying it.

(10) Without Anger: In conclusion, *akrodha* means no anger. Whatever may happen there should be no anger in the mind. To discipline someone in anger is one thing, but when anger overwhelms the mind we become slaves of it. Do not be an instrument in the hands of anger, as a slave is in the hands of the dictator who rules him! We should have perfect control over anger and also have the discrimination to know when and where to show anger, if necessary.

The last point to emphasize here is that our attempt must be to follow and practice these values in full measure—one hundred percent! In other activities, a sixty or eighty percent job may be good enough, but not when it comes to living our principles. If our honesty is only eighty percent and our dishonesty is twenty percent, we are not really honest persons! We must live these kinds of values completely and not just in part.

Also, we should never complain "Those people are not following these value's, so why should I?" Just as we would not take poison merely because another person has; do not be affected with what other people are or are not doing. We can be concerned only with whether or not we are following the right values in life. We have to perfect our own lives, and in this, we must strive hard.

XI

Vegetarianism

A question often asked by people concerns vegetarianism and non-vegetarianism. This is a relevant topic because it involves the value of *ahiṃsā,* which is one aspect of *sanātana dharma.*

What is the position of *Manu Smṛti* on the question of eating meat? The general commandment given (called a *sāmānya*) is: "Do not eat meat." There are a number of reasons why this injunction is given. One is from the spiritual standpoint, that there is one Self or one Life that pulsates in all beings; since all beings want to live happily in this world, we do not have the moral right to take away a life or to cause any unhappiness or sorrow to others. This is a simple *dharma* to understand.

The second reason is that the greatness and dignity of human beings is their ability to sacrifice their lives for others. The person who sacrifices his comforts or wealth, his happiness, or even his life, in order to protect, sustain, and help others, is considered great. Therefore, if we destroy other beings for the sake of our own pleasure, we are cutting the very root of the glory of human life and degrading ourselves.

Recently, organizations have been formed to protect wildlife and forestry. A movement of this kind is necessary nowadays because there are so many greedy and cruel people who are concerned only with their own money and pleasure and who are ready to destroy anything for their own sakes. Human beings should sacrifice for others, not sacrifice others for their own personal comforts, pleasures, or other pursuits.

A third reason for not eating meat is given with respect to an argument put forth by some non-vegetarians: If all beings have life and vegetarians are killing and eating plant-life, why should we not eat animals also? However this argument is really a fallacious one, for if we extend this reasoning a little further, we would then be asking why we cannot eat human beings also. If it is necessary to destroy life no matter what we eat, then why not kill our old people when there is a shortage of food? But, of course, everyone would reply, "Oh, that is horrible! How can you say that?" No one will agree with the argument when it is taken that far.

Even though there is life in all beings, in both the vegetable and animal kingdoms, there are degrees of evolution and of the manifestation of intelligence. The degree of feeling and understanding, of mental and physical pain, is much less developed in plant-life as compared to animal-life. According to our *dharma śāstra*, the purpose of human life is to know the Truth. In order to know the Truth, we must sustain our lives, but it needs to be done with proper discrimination.

When a patient goes to a doctor, the doctor will try to treat the patient with as little medicine as possible and without an operation. However, if an operation is necessary, the doctor performs it generally with anesthesia, so as to give the least amount of harm and discomfort to the patient.

In the same way, although life must be sustained with life, it should be done by causing the least pain and disturbance to nature. This means that even when eating vegetarian food we should eat moderately and with discrimination. Even from an anatomical point of view, the body-structure of a carnivorous animal is meant for eating meat whereas the human body is not. From a medical standpoint also many people today are advised to reduce their fat and cholesterol intake, which generally means the reduction of red meat in the diet. It is needless to explain here that not only meat-eating, but excessive eating of any kind is not good for physical health.

Injunctions and Concessions

When we hear these scriptural injunctions, we may wonder whether people were eating meat in the Vedic period. Yes, people were eating meat then, as they are now, and they also will be in the future. Under certain circumstances even the Vedas and *dharma śāstra* gave this permission. But an important distinction should be clear: that we should not eat meat is the injunction given to us and it is our *dharma*. The permission to eat meat in other situations is only a concession due to our human weaknesses, which sometimes make us incapable of living up to a higher ideal.

The purpose of the scriptures in giving this concession may be illustrated by the following example. Suppose a person who is highly diabetic goes to a doctor. Ordinarily, the doctor's prescription will be to forbid the patient to have any sweets at all, for this is the correct *dharma* for the patient and is the best remedy for his physical health. However, if the doctor knows that the patient has a strong craving for sweets and by forbidding them completely the patient will most likely eat them on the sly, the intelligent doctor tells the patient, "All right, you can eat sweets once a month." Therefore, in this case, the permission to eat sweets once a month is not an injunction but a concession.

In the same way, people in the world develop strong desires or cravings for things, and when they are suddenly prohibited from having them, there is a tendency to revolt against those injunctions and to find illegal or wrong ways of obtaining and enjoying the things they want. Therefore, in order to control their urges and desires, the *dharma śāstra* sometimes gives concessions for the highly *tamasic* people. Yet, at the same time, the *śāstra* places many conditions on a particular action. It explains, for instance, which animals can be eaten, the days of the month when eating meat is prohibited, and what special rituals are to be performed before eating. But the very fact that so many restrictions are laid down shows that the ideal in the *śāstra* is to rise above this craving.

Non-vegetarian food was also allowed for a particular class of people, the *kṣatriyas*, rulers of kingdoms. For other classes, such as the business people (*vaiśyas*) or the philosophers/teachers (*brahmins*), hunting and eating meat were not allowed. Why was this distinction made? Because the *kṣatriyas*' type of work required that they have the courage to fight to protect the nation. They underwent training in defense (hunting) and needed animal protein for physical strength.

Even today this science of training and diet will be appreciated by the medical field, as doctors prescribe different diets for different people, depending on the type of work they do or the need to correct a vitamin deficiency. People with tendencies for spiritual or scholarly studies were not allowed to eat meat because the mind needs to be very quiet and subtle for this type of work, whereas the *kṣatriya* warriors needed a lot of *rajo guṇa* (passionate-active nature) to have the ambition and ability to fight. Yet the *kṣatriyas* were told that after a certain age even they should renounce that type of life, take *sannyāsa* (the order of renunciation), and go to the forest for contemplation.

In summary, the injunction given in the scriptures is not to eat meat; and when special permission is given to eat it, this is only a concession depending on the nature of the seeker, the time, the place, and so on. The main point is that we should not be confused as to which is the injunction and which is the concession. This, in fact, is the greatness of the scriptures—they understand the weakness of the human mind and are able to give instructions according to individual needs.

XII

The Four Stages of Life

In the context of our present discussion, the meaning of *āśrama* is "a stage in life." Our Hindu scriptures describe four stages: the *brahmacarya āśrama* (the student's life), *gṛhastha āśrama* (the householder's life), *vānaprastha āśrama* (the life of retirement or preparatory renunciation), and the *sannyāsa āśrama* (the renounced order of life). No real *vānaprastha* stage exists today because no one knows what to do in their old age except retire, go to an old-age home, and watch television all day!

Our Hindu scriptures, however, are very scientific. Considering a human being's life to be 100 years maximum, the life span is divided roughly into four stages of twenty-five years each. Student life goes up to twenty-five years, the householder up to fifty years, *vānaprastha* up to seventy-five years, and so on. In fact, it is said that when you see the face of your grandson, you should retire for contemplation. Then there will be no generation gap problem! Remember, though one may criticize the older generation now, no matter how modern one thinks oneself to be at this moment, the next generation will also consider you an old and outdated person! Thus the scriptures say that before this happens, one should leave the house and prepare for renunciation. Then after *vānaprastha*, one should take *sannyāsa*, the complete renunciation of all worldly affairs, and have total devotion to spiritual knowledge alone. This is the general scheme for the *varṇāśramas*.

Prescribed Duties

For each *āśrama* or stage of life, particular duties are prescribed in the *sastra*.

Brahmacarya: The Student's Life. We read in the traditional accounts of how the student goes to live and study with the teacher performing *muṇḍana* (shaving of the head), *homa* (sacrifice), and *havana* (daily sacrificial rituals). Though we may say that all this is irrelevant now, we should know that the underlying value holds as true today as it did then. The main principle enunciated for the disciple was: "If you are a *vidyārthī* (one who is a seeker of knowledge alone), you must give up the idea of comforts." On the other hand, the scriptures say: "But if you are a seeker of comforts, then forget about knowledge," for it will not come to you.

In this so-called industrial civilization, the situation is as the latter statement indicates. Due to the smaller family units, the children get pampered with all kinds of comforts and possessions and fight each other for them. The children become glued to the television, and rather than becoming more intelligent, statistics show us that those who watch more television actually have lower I.Q.s, while those children who watch less television do better in their studies. The fact is that when a student chases after clothes, food, pleasures, and comforts, there is no time for study and concentration, and the mind becomes dissipated.

The scriptures tell us that the first duty of the student is to be totally devoted to study and knowledge, to have devotion and respect for the teacher, as well as for the books of study. These days when students go out to sit on the lawn, if there is nothing else to sit on, they take out their books and sit on them! The student should also make no other demands on the family. If a student wants a car, for example, he/she should work to earn it.

The students in the *brahmacarya āśrama* were also taught the eternal values of life (*sanātana dharma*), which we have already discussed. They were taught the ultimate goal of life and how to prepare for it. Having learned the universal and general values of living, the students would then choose their own professions and train in that particular field—just as today the university students take general courses first, followed by specialized courses in their chosen field. Children of royal families, for instance, were taught political science, economics, warfare, and other related sciences.

Thereafter the students were ready for the next stage of life, the householder's life. It is said in *Taittirīya Upaniṣad*: "Having given *dakṣiṇā* (gift) to your teacher, in the form of that which is most dear to him (and to you), do not cut off the line of descendants." (I:11) Out of gratitude we should give to the teacher *priya dhana*, which means that which is not only dear to the teacher but also what is dear to us, because often we keep what is dear to us and give away only what we do not like!

After having taken permission from the teacher, one was free to enter into the householder's life. Today we find these nobler ideas disappearing from the student's life, as the problem of dating is coming up more. Young Indians ask me angrily, "Swamiji, why do our parents prevent us from dating? We want to go to parties and other things." But then the very purpose of the student's life is defeated—the mind becomes completely distracted. Boy and girl meet each other and fall in love; they become infatuated with each other for some time, but later one of them goes away and the other is left shattered. Love is gone, study is gone, and knowledge is gone! I remind them that their whole life is before them to do all the things they want. Reserve the precious early years wholly for study and come to lead a fulfilling life.

Thus, the students must devote their entire energy to educate themselves—not only to read and write, but also to lay a strong foundation for the moral, ethical, cultural, and spiritual aspects of life. Aside from academic training, our educational systems must give students a higher ideal for which to strive. The students must become the makers of their own destiny and of the nation's destiny also. This is their great responsibility.

The Householder's Life

Marriages are also of different types. When people ask me whether an arranged marriage or a love-marriage is best, I say, "A successful marriage is best!" Successful marriages have nothing to do with being arranged because there are examples of success and failure in both types of marriages. The main point is that there should be mutual love, respect, and readiness to sacrifice for each other. This is the ideal of the householder's life, and when both partners have this ideal in mind, the marriage is successful; but if each person is only demanding from the other there will always be a problem.

There are many duties or *kartavya karmas* prescribed for the householder's life. Though we cannot discuss them in detail here, one very important point should be brought out, which is given in the *śāstra*: "In those houses where the women are honored and respected, the gods dwell there. Where the women are not respected and honored, whatever one does is futile." In other words, if the lady of the house is unhappy or abused in any way, no work will bring fulfillment or prosperity to that house. Another verse says: "The husband must see that the wife is happy and the wife must see that the husband is happy. When both are making each other happy, there will be auspiciousness and welfare for all in that house."

This is the ideal for the householder's life, and if this ideal is not held by both husband and wife, there will only be fighting between them; and when the children see this repeatedly, they will also fight. Such a household will be filled with violence. We see this catastrophe happening nowadays as the number of broken families, unwed mothers, single parent homes, and other such problems increase. These problems will also exist in the future as long as a person is only demanding from others.

Another instruction given to the householder concerns food: "Do not censure food, do not waste food, grow more food." Food also represents general wealth and prosperity; therefore the significance is that material prosperity should neither be criticized nor wasted, but should be cultivated and shared with others, not used for that one household alone. In the *Taittirīya Upaniṣad*, it is said:

> *Do not turn away anybody who seeks shelter and lodging. This is the vow. Let one, therefore, acquire much food by any means*

> *whatsoever. One should say, "Food is ready." If the food is prepared in the best manner, the food is given to him (the host) also in the best manner. If the food is prepared in a mediocre manner, food is also given to him (the host) in a mediocre manner. If food is prepared in the lowest manner, the same food is also given to him (the host). He who knows thus, will obtain all the rewards as mentioned above.* (III:10)

Here it is said that when a guest comes to the house, he should not be refused, but we should offer him a comfortable seat and offer food with respect. The Upanishad also tells us that when we give food to a guest with respect, we will likewise be given things with respect; but if we give food to someone in an insulting or casual way, the same will be returned to us.

It is also the duty of the householders to take care of the *brahmacārīs* and *sannyāsīs*. In fact, the *Manu Smṛti* clearly says that among the four *āśramas,* the householder's life is supreme because all the other three depend upon the householder to take care of and maintain their welfare.

When all of the above instructions are taken into consideration, the householder's life becomes meaningful. Yet, at the same time, the householder must not become drowned in this type of living; he should continue to have the company of holy people (*satsaṅga*) and slowly prepare his mind for the next stage of life. The purpose of the householder's life, therefore, is not to get stuck in the household but to slowly rise above it and expand his vision with higher Knowledge—to become one with the universe. This preparation is called the *vānaprastha āśrama.*

Thus the householder's duties are manifold, as we have seen. If one keeps these essential principles in mind, one's specific duties will also become self-evident. It is not enough that the parents produce children (*prajā*). Their responsibility extends to make sure their children are *suprajā*, a noble generation. More time must be given to this aspect of family life. Generally, a householder's time is spent in earning money. But it is much more important to make a noble person than to make money, for a noble person will bring all kinds of prosperity in the future—material and spiritual—to himself, his family, and to the society. By serving relatives and those in the other three *āśramas*, the householder must expand his or her vision of family and learn to rise above ego and personal, selfish interests.

Vānaprastha Āśrama

Having prepared ourselves for life with the knowledge gained as a student and having tested that knowledge and allowed it to mature within us through the *gṛhastha's* life of duties, the *vānaprastha* stage comes next. In this *āśrama* one slowly withdraws from hectic, worldly activities and devotes more time to spirituality. In earlier times, the husband would leave the home and go to the forest with or without his wife, depending on whether she was ready to accompany him.

In *Rāmacaritamānasa*, by Saint Tulsidas, it is said that Manu, the *svayambhuvarāja* (world-progenitor of the age), told his wife, Shatarupa, "Now I am retiring to the forest." But she was one step ahead of him and replied, "I have been waiting for this day, wondering why you had not left earlier. I am going with you." Together they went to the forest for contemplation. It is said that the two never interfered any longer in household affairs and gave advice to their children only if they came and asked for it.

As *vānaprasthas*, the husband and wife do not have the same relationship as before; they relate to each other only as seekers of Truth, as friends going together to the Lord. In this way, more time can be spent in spiritual practices, in preparation for *sannyāsa*.

Sannyāsa Āśrama

The final stage is the *sannyāsa āśrama*, the life of total renunciation. But the important question is: What does one renounce?

When a person is initiated into *sannyāsa*, a sacrifice called *viraja homa* is done. The most significant part of this *homa* is the point at which the initiate repeats aloud: "*Sannyasto mayā, sannyasto mayā, sannyasto mayā*," meaning "I have renounced, I have renounced, I have renounced." This triple repetition can represent a number of things: that I have no more identification with my gross body, subtle body (mind and intellect), or with my causal body (the unmanifest *vāsanās*); or the three can represent the waking, dream, and deep-sleep states—having renounced my identification with them. The three can also mean that I no longer have any desire for things in this world, in the lower worlds, or in the higher, heavenly worlds—for progeny, for money, or for name and fame. In short, I renounce everything.

But what is the essence of this *sannyāsa*? It is the total renunciation of desire and of all "littleness." Whenever we use the word "renounce," we generally associate some kind of pain with it. We ask the *sannyāsī* with surprise, "Have you really left your house?" But the *sannyāsī* answers, "No, I have only left this one little house so I can embrace the world. Instead of calling this one place my home, I now call the whole world my home. In fact, the world is me, myself!" To see the world as one's own Self is true *sannyāsa*.

The *sannyāsa āśrama* also results in fearlessness (*abhayatva*). Society fears an ordinary person who is full of desires because there is always a possibility that he may take away another person's wealth; but the *sannyāsī* has no more desires and so he can honestly say to society, "Now you need not be afraid of me." He is no longer afraid of society, the world, or even of death.

A *sannyāsī*'s life is meant wholly for seeking Truth; it is for serving others and not for receiving services from others. The *sannyāsa āśrama* is essentially the giving up of all "I-ness" and "my-ness." It is for the realization of the Self.

The normal order in which one proceeds through the stages of life are: from *brahmacarya* to *gṛhastha* to *vānaprastha* to *sannyāsa āśrama*. However, our *śāstras* say that if there is a person who even at the student's stage of life has extreme dispassion and desire for Knowledge alone, whether boy or girl, that person can go directly to the *sannyāsa āśrama* without having to pass through the other stages. A famous statement in the Upanishads declares: "That very day when you develop dispassion, do not wait (to leave the house)."

If a person is unmarried and wants to take *sannyāsa*, he must ask permission from his parents. If married, one must ask permission from one's spouse. In extreme cases, however, when the dispassion is very strong, it will not be considered wrong if one takes any steps to get *sannyāsa*, providing it is out of a desire for Knowledge alone.

XIII

The Four Castes

The next topic to be discussed is the *varṇa dharma*, the duties prescribed for each caste. The word "caste" is a problem for many people today because over time, the whole idea has come to be entirely misunderstood.

In Sanskrit, *varṇa* means to describe or that by which a thing is described. *Varṇa* can also mean name, color, form, quality, relationship, and so on, because we describe a thing according to these attributes. When we study a science, botany or zoology for instance, the entire vegetable and animal kingdoms are classified according to similar qualities and attributes. The same is true in the material sciences such as physics and chemistry, where elements and minerals of similar properties are grouped together.

Among human beings there is also much variety in color, shape, ability, mental temperament, and so on. When we say that all human beings are equal, we mean this to be true from the spiritual standpoint, in that each one has capacity to do something, whatever it may be. Each one has a particular ability by nature: One person performs physical labor, another writes poetry, or does public speaking, and yet another does social service work. Thus just as objects and beings are classified in other sciences according to their different natures, spiritual science also classifies society into four groups, the *catur varṇa*. These four types of people are found everywhere in the world, not just in India. In this regard, Lord Krishna makes a famous statement in the *Bhagavad Gītā,* which says:

> *The four-fold caste has been created by Me according to the differentiation of* guṇa *(quality) and* karma *(action).* (IV:13)

There must always be a basis for classifications. For example, countries of the world are classified as "third-world countries," "developed nations," or "underdeveloped nations." But what is the standard of measurement here? From what standpoint is one country considered developed or underdeveloped? Because if we look from a spiritual standpoint, those that are considered materially underdeveloped might be the most developed spiritually. The *catur varṇa* are classified based on *guṇa* and *karma.*

Caste Based on Karma

(1) *Brahmins* (the thinking class): With respect to this first category, *karma* would mean one's ability to study, research, invent, discover, teach, and do other such work that requires much thought. Everyone is not able to do this. Just as we see the number of dropouts from secular schools increasing, the same is true in the spiritual field. For example, for the two-year Vedanta course at Sandeepany, Bombay, we receive about 500 applications; 200 of those applicants appear for the interview; out of those 200, about 80 are selected. Of those eighty, only about forty students actually join the course; and after joining, the teacher is lucky to be left with twenty students by the end of the two-year program. When those twenty are asked at the conclusion, "Now how many of you are ready to work in the field," maybe twelve to fifteen students will want to work and propagate this knowledge. This does not mean, of course, that those who drop out are useless or inferior—it only means that their capacities are better used in other fields or occupations.

From Vedic times onwards, those who were of an intellectual nature, capable of studying and teaching, were called *brahmins*, the thinking class. This is why every organization always has an advisory board—a "think tank"—to create new ideas and make decisions.

(2) *Kṣatriyas* (the leader class): The second category is capable of leading the society towards the ideals shown by the *brahmins*, of looking after the people and of courageously fighting battles when necessary. Though the "thinker" has visions or ideals for society, he does not always have the capacity to bring them about in a practical way. Hence the *kṣatriya* is needed, as this type of person can act on the ideas. The *kṣatriyas* are the natural-born leaders of society.

(3) *Vaiśyas* (the business class): The third category, that of the *vaiśyas*, have a propensity to produce wealth, not only for themselves but for society at large. These are the people engaged in agriculture, cattle-raising, and other businesses. We all know that not everybody has this business tendency and know-how.

(4) *Śūdras* (the labor class): The fourth category is made up of those who perform service (*sevā*). They are not capable of thinking of ideas, leading the society, or producing much wealth, but when they are told what needs to be done, they will do it. Therefore, in every organization, there are people who give suggestions and make plans, others who put the plans into action, others who do the fund-raising, and still others who do whatever practical labor needs to be done.

The main point is that everybody is capable of doing one thing or another, and no category is in any way inferior to another. In fact, when you understand the real meaning of the four *varṇas*, you will see that each of us is really a *brahmin*, *kṣatriya*, *vaiśya*, and *śūdra*, all put together in one! Personally, I find this true: in one field I am able to have an idea or vision, but am not able to do anything practically, whereas in another field I am able to work, but do not have creative ideas. Practically speaking, all four types are necessary in our individual lives, in the family units, and in social activities. Yet a person is called a *brahmin*, *kṣatriya*, *vaiśya*, or *śūdra* depending on whether his or her nature is predominantly that of a thinker, leader, business person, or worker.

Caste According to Guṇa

As Lord Krishna explained in the *Bhagavad Gītā*, the classification of castes is also based on one's inner mental qualities or *guṇas*. It is said that human nature and all nature (*prakṛti*) is composed of three *guṇas*: *sattva*, *rajas*, and *tamas*.

Sattvoguṇa is of the nature of knowledge: a desire for knowledge and the qualities of love, faith, kindness, and compassion. The *rajoguṇa* is of the nature of activity. Numerous desires and ambitions are its manifestations. *Tamas* is of the nature of inertia, and it manifests as dullness and little interest or ambition of any kind.

A *brahmin* is described as one who is predominantly *sāttvic*, with some *rajas* and a little *tamas* in his personality. A *kṣatriya* is one who is predominantly *rājasic*, a very ambitious person, with some *sattva* and a little *tamas* in him. A *vaiśya* is one in whom the *guṇa* of *rajas* is predominant, yet with almost as much *tamas* and the least amount of *sattvoguṇa*. The *śūdra* is predominantly *tāmasic*, with some *rajas* and very little *sattva*.

In conclusion, we have seen that the division of the *varṇa āśramas* is based on action (*karma*) and quality (*guṇa*)—not on birth (*janma*), as is commonly understood today. In fact, the *Manu Smṛti* says that everyone is actually born as a *śūdra* (*janmanā jāyate śūdraḥ*) because at birth we are basically the raw material of life, from which anything can be made. We cannot judge what a person will be by what caste he is born into, for a *brahmin* can become a *śūdra* and a *śūdra* can become a *brahmin*. Some people live an inspired life in their youth, but later on become dull and debased. While others begin life by being dull, but become very bright and successful later on.

How, then, did this caste-by-birth system come about? This has happened only in the last several hundred years, when people with *brahmin* qualities, for instance, began to marry only those people with similar qualities. Children born into such a family were then called *brahmins*. However, this was not the original intent nor the basis upon which the *varṇas* were actually divided. As it is said in the *Cāṇakya Sūtra*, "A person should be engaged only in a field of activity that he is capable of doing."

When this principle is followed there is no problem. Furthermore, if everyone has the attitude that I am capable of doing this particular work and am doing it to serve the society, then naturally there will be *dharma*, the total integration of society as well as of the individual. If we do not have this understanding, disintegration will be the only result.

Devotion to One's Duty

As explained earlier, *dharma* is that which integrates the individual as well as society and enables one to ultimately reach the true *dharma*, abidance in the absolute nature of the Self. Whether one is capable of thinking and planning, of leading, creating wealth, or doing manual labor, *dharma* is fulfilled when people of all four castes, or *varṇas*, perform their duties and responsibilities completely in an attitude of selflessness. In the field of education, for instance, if the students are sincerely interested in their studies, if the teachers are devoted to their profession, and if the administration is devoted to its own task, the schools will run smoothly. At home, if mother, father, and children all fulfill their duties devotedly, there will be sweetness and peace in the house, but if everyone argues and wants to give up their own duty, saying, "Why do I have to do this, why do you not do it?" there will only be friction. Disharmony comes about only when we are careless and forgetful of our duties. In the *Bhagavad Gītā*, Lord Krishna says: "Engaged in one's own duty, one attains perfection." (XVIII:45)

Devotion to duty gives us purity of mind and this purity brings about inner perfection and complete Self-unfoldment. A doctor does not have to do the work of a lawyer, and a lawyer does not have to do the work of an engineer. Each one should remain devoted to the work of which he is capable. Perfection of a worldly kind too, even national fame, is attainable by one who devotes his or her entire energy to his or her special field of interest and talent.

Dedicated Action

With what attitude should we perform our work? The Lord tells us in the *Gītā*:

> *He from whom all beings have evolved, by whom all this world is pervaded, worshiping Him with one's own duty, one attains perfection.* (XVIII:46)

Whatever work we do should be looked upon as duty and should be done as worship of the Lord in an attitude of dedication and surrender. Which Lord should we worship? We should worship that supreme Lord from whom this entire world has emerged and by whom this entire world is pervaded. Work done with this attitude of worship of the infinite Lord is called true *karma*.

To understand how dedicated action integrates society, let us take an example of how a good cup of coffee is made. First we must have the four ingredients: water, coffee powder, milk, and sugar. The nature of the water is not that of the powder; the nature of the powder is not the same as the sugar. Each ingredient has its own special quality. We cannot say that one ingredient is more important than the other. Here there is no question of superiority or inferiority. But when all four ingredients are mixed together in proper proportion and each ingredient surrenders or offers its quality for the sake of the whole, then that coffee is wonderful! Imagine if the coffee powder says, "I am superior! Why should I surrender?" and it decides to withdraw its quality! The result will be no coffee at all.

Society is something like this cup of coffee. It is made up of its four ingredients, the four castes, and each one has its own nature, its own special contribution to make to the whole. None is superior to the other. If each individual becomes dedicated to offer his or her own best qualities in serving others, the result will be a better society.

Problems in society arise only when we assume a mistaken sense of superiority and inferiority. Though in India they say problems are because of the caste system, we find that the same kinds of pressures exist almost everywhere, in communist, capitalist, or socialist countries, whether or not the divisions of people are called *brahmins*, *kṣatriyas*, and so on. If it is not a problem of caste, it may be due to racial discrimination or something else. When individuals or racial groups think themselves superior to others, they will want to exercise authority over the other parties. This may continue for some time. But how long will the oppressed remain suppressed and controlled? Sooner or later they will revolt and a struggle of some kind will ensue, sometimes even leading to war.

Remember, it is not that something is necessarily wrong with the social or political system. The system can only work properly when all its component parts work in harmony and with dedication. The present degraded condition in India and everywhere else in the world is due only to humanity's greed, selfishness, pride, arrogance, and other such negative qualities.

In summary, *varṇa āśrama dharma* is the fulfillment of all our duties given to us according to our station or stage in life, performed in an attitude of worship, and offered to the Lord for the benefit of the entire society. Though this topic could be discussed in much more detail, each person can take this much and reflect upon it deeply.

XIV

The Purpose of Religious Festivals

Our next topic of discussion is India's religious festivals. What is the need for them? How are they celebrated? What is their significance and how can we make the best use of these occasions?

Let us first analyze why there is a need for these religious festivals. As we work everyday from morning until evening, we become tired and naturally need to rest. We go home to eat and sleep and we feel revitalized, and are ready to work again the next morning. However, as our life continues between work and rest, day after day, a kind of monotony sets in. We feel bored and think to ourselves, "I need a change." Although our physical exhaustion is revived by sleeping, how do we get rid of this boredom, this mental exhaustion? What we generally do is look for some kind of entertainment.

The Sanskrit word for entertainment, *mano rañjana,* means delighting the mind, entertaining the mind. Some people sit and watch television for entertainment, others play cards, go on picnics, or spend time on a hobby. Everyone looks forward to their weekends so that they can do something that is fun and relaxing, a relief from the pressure and monotony of work. Yet after a while, even these weekends become routine and we want to go on vacations to Lake Tahoe, Disney World, or Las Vegas! When even these places become dull for us, we want to go to other exotic countries far away from our ordinary experiences—some place totally different! Thus our vacations and amusements are meant to remove our boredom and give us a sense of mental rest and relaxation, at least for some time.

Recognizing this need for change and entertainment, the Hindu religion provides special occasions, festivals of a religious nature, called *utsava*. No religion will last very long if it does not understand the common needs and desires of people, insisting only on strict discipline at all times. Aside from fasting there must also be feasting, singing, dancing, and joyous celebration.

One may ask that if the purpose of these festivals is to remove our mental and physical exhaustion, then why are our vacations and weekends not sufficient? Why do we need religious festivals that involve *pūjās*? The answer is clear: Though these various amusements relax the mind and revive us for a while, they themselves become monotonous rituals after some time, leaving us with a peculiar feeling of incompleteness afterwards. Although the purpose of vacations is to help us feel rested, to gain more enthusiasm, cheerfulness and energy for our regular work, we generally find that the opposite is true. When the vacation is over, we think, "Oh, now I have to go back to the office. What a bore!" Often we are left exhausted not only physically, but also financially! Our pockets are empty and we must again work hard to make up for the lost hard-earned money. The pleasure of the vacation has, in effect, not removed the pressure, it only added a new one! Why did the vacation not give us the desired result? Because it is purposeless entertainment.

On the other hand, our religious festivals have a very different effect. They not only give us occasions for merrymaking, but they also give us a noble, divine vision and inspire us to raise our mind to the heights of that great goal. Rather than merely exhausting us physically and mentally, they purify the mind and prepare us to face life with more enthusiasm, to live life more happily and fully. If we observe these festivals closely, we will see that they not only point out the ultimate goal of life, but also give us the guidelines to reach that goal. In short, our religious festivals serve the purpose of all other entertainment and at the same time give us much more.

Varieties of Festivals

Hindu religious festivals can be classified into several different groups. Some celebrate the birth of great incarnations of the Lord, such as Sri Ramachandra and Sri Krishna. Similar festivals glorify the life and work of divine masters. Other festivals relate to the change of seasons. For example, Makarasankranti, usually celebrated in January, is fixed at the time when the sun changes its course and begins moving northward again. Vasantapancami (*vasanta* meaning spring) marks the beginning of the spring season. By celebrating these seasonal changes we are made more aware of the changes in nature. The dominant idea behind these festivals is that we should live more in harmony with nature instead of trying to destroy her and make her our slave.

Holi, the festival of colors, is another great seasonal festival, celebrated especially in North India. At this time, everybody splashes colored water or powder all over each other—on faces, clothes, everything! It is wonderful because it reflects exactly what is occurring in nature at that time—when all the beautiful flowers of different colors are blossoming! By celebrating this event we feel a greater oneness with nature. This splashing of colors was also a famous *līlā* (pastime) in Sri Krishna's life.

Other festivals, such as Onam (in Kerala) or Baisaki, celebrate the harvest time, a time of plenty, signifying both material and spiritual prosperity. Navaratri and Divali (the festival of lights) celebrate the victory of good over evil. In addition, we also have national festivals, such as Independence Day, which are associated with great national heroes who led very inspiring lives. Though these festivals are not religious in nature, still they set before us a higher goal and encourage us to work hard in that direction. Finally, there are the *adhyātmic* (highly subjective in nature) festivals, including Shivaratri.

I will now explain some important aspects that are similar in the festivals of Sri Rama Navami, Sri Krishna Janmashtami, and Maha Shivaratri.

Sri Rama Navami generally comes toward the end of March or beginning of April and is celebrated at noon. Long ago, when the wicked king Ravana ruled in Lanka, the good people were being persecuted by him and unrighteousness prevailed. The suffering people prayed to God for help. Soon He was born on earth as the Prince of Ayodhya to destroy evildoers and to establish the kingdom of righteousness. This is the *avatāra* or incarnation of Sri Rama.

Sri Krishna Janmashtami comes in late August or early September and celebrates the midnight birth of Lord Krishna. Lord Krishna also incarnated for the purpose of destroying evil and restoring righteousness on earth.

The great festival of Maha Shivaratri celebrates the appearance of Lord Shiva at midnight in the form of a column of light (*jyoti*).

The important point to be noted in the celebration of these festivals is the sequence of their three phases: the preparation before the appearance of the Lord, the Lord's actual appearance or incarnation, and the final joyous celebration after his arrival. Each of these phases is of deep spiritual significance.

Preparation

Before the actual moment of the Lord's birth, people generally observe a fast as a way of preparing for the Lord's coming. This fast has two aspects: one is the withdrawal from indulgence in sensual pleasures. Fasting means not just abstinence from food, but from sense objects of all kinds, for we are constantly eating through all our sense organs. We eat forms and colors through our eyes, sounds through our ears, fragrances through our nose, and so on. When we eat all these sense objects through their respective sense organs, what we are actually feeding is the mind. The mind grows or breeds on these sense perceptions and thereafter runs constantly outward in their direction and becomes totally dissipated. True fasting, therefore, is to have control over the sense organs and to cease from indulgence in sense pleasures.

The second important aspect in the observance of a fast is to constantly be chanting the name of the Lord, to think of Him, to worship, meditate, and pray to Him. The Sanskrit word for fasting, *upavāsa*, comes from *upa* meaning near and *vas* meaning to live. Thus, fasting reminds us to "sit near" the Lord mentally. For this reason devotees will often do their *japa* (repetition of the Lord's name) and *pūjā* while sitting near a picture or image of the Lord with a lamp burning in front of it. The purpose of this is to purify the mind and to be ardently praying to Him, "O Lord, please manifest Thyself in my heart!"

Manifestation

The manifestation of the Lord takes place in two ways. Objectively, Sri Ramachandraji actually did take birth in the city of Ayodhya and lived an exemplary life in order to teach everyone the *dharmic* way of living. This is one aspect of the manifestation that we celebrate. The other is the subjective manifestation that occurs when the mind and intellect are totally integrated and perfectly tuned with the Divine. Generally our mind is constantly wandering in many different directions and toward many different objects. Numerous thoughts are constantly rising. Therefore, the pure Consciousness, which is the eternal substratum of all thought, is not recognized by us. But when the mind is withdrawn from all objects and made single-pointed through meditation, there comes a point when the last thought has ended and no new thought has risen. At this juncture the mind is called *nirviṣayamanas*, meaning thoughtless or objectless mind. This objectless mind is pure Awareness itself and its recognition is called realization, the birth of the Lord in the heart.

This is, in fact, the significance of the timing of many incarnations of the Lord. At midday, when Sri Ramachandra was born, the morning had ended and the afternoon had not yet begun. At midnight, when Lord Krishna was born and Lord Shiva manifested Himself, one day was over and the next day had not yet begun. This juncture or midpoint between two periods of time is called *sandhikāla* and it represents this objectless state of mind, when realization of the pure Consciousness, which is the Self, takes place within us.

Celebration

During their lifetimes, both Sri Ramachandra and Sri Krishna destroyed evildoers and reestablished the kingdom of righteousness and happiness in the world. In the same way, when realization takes place within, one recognizes one's own true Self. All ignorance and ignorance-created delusions, all negative tendencies of the mind, get totally destroyed. Thereafter, one lives ever in the experience of the blissful Self, the kingdom of joy. This joy of realization is represented externally in the festivals by the lighting of lamps everywhere, by singing and dancing, and by the distribution of sweets (Divali)!

These three phases of the religious festivals—preparation, incarnation, and celebration—represent the three phases of spiritual progress. Our preparation consists of first purifying the mind by withdrawing it from sense objects, then making it single-pointed by turning it toward the Lord in *japa* and meditation. When the mind is fully prepared and all thoughts have ended, the Self—which is of the nature of pure Consciousness—is recognized. When the ego has been completely destroyed, life is forever a joyous celebration in the bliss of the Self!

Shivaratri

The great festival of Maha Shivaratri, which we generally celebrate in the month of February, follows this same three-phase sequence. On Shivaratri Day, devotees fast completely and hold onto the one thought of the Lord by chanting continuously, "*Om Namaḥ Śivāya*," meaning salutations to Lord Shiva. The mind is held in single-pointed concentration until the stroke of midnight, when it is said that Lord Shiva manifests Himself as the light of Consciousness within.

As explained in the context of the Navaratri festival, the celebration at night signifies our waking up from the sleep of ignorance into the state of absolute Knowledge. At the present moment we know only two states—the mind when it is extrovert and the mind when in deep sleep. The extrovert mind is conscious of and indulges in the world outside through the five sense organs. The mind in deep sleep is in a state of total ignorance, completely unaware of the world. We do not yet know that state wherein the mind is withdrawn from the world yet fully awake to Reality. This is why, on Shivaratri, one is supposed to stay awake all night—in order to practice the simultaneous withdrawal of the mind from the sense objects, as we do in sleep, and yet keep the mind in a state of alert awareness. In this state of objectless Awareness comes the moment of spiritual awakening, the true Shivaratri!

PART FOUR

The Epics

Scriptures provide
the Science of Life
and the Art of Living.

Swami Chinmayananda

The *Rāmāyaṇa* supplied the rich melody that modulated the heart and molded the muscles of the Indian culture. Spiritual glory, mystical quiet, moral splendor, and physical valor are the essential stamp of Hindu life. All these were at once generated, nourished, and kept blazing in the Indian character, through the constant study of this world-famous epic. Even now it can repeat its magic. Rama, the perfect ideal, is made to play life on a stage as filthy as the world that is the common lot of all of us. Crisscrossing through its exhaustive drama are the tensions of passions, emotions, jealousies, pride, lust, greed, the madness of power, the hunger for wealth, the thirst for pleasure, and the delusions of attachments.

There are the tender narrations of innocent childhood, heroic descriptions of irrepressible youth, and learned discourses upon the wisdom of old age. In short, the *Rāmāyaṇa* is a picture gallery, where each picture is perfect, and yet the entire gallery is confusing with its own variegated colors and rich profusion, just like the picture of the world about us. In and through them all, Sri Rama stands out, bearing His righteous bow, ever in the defense of honor and truth, of justice and peace. He also has a dash of frailties, which make Him truly human, and yet, in His divine glories He stands out distinctly, a colossus of beauty, a mighty titan of strength, and a soaring peak of Olympus.

Swami Chinmayananda

XV

Itihāsa and Purāṇas

We will now discuss the two categories of literature called *Itihāsa* and *Purāṇa*, commonly translated as history and mythology, respectively. The two themes of *dharma* and *Brahma vidyā,* dealt with in the Vedas (*śruti* and *smṛti granthas*), are elaborated upon in these two books of literature.

The literal meaning of *Itihāsa* is *iti ha āsa*: Thus it was, we have heard (by tradition). These historical events took place in the distant past and because we have not seen them ourselves, we know them only by what has been reported to us by others. *Hāsa* also means laughter and *iti* can mean death or end. Who has the last laugh in this world? Lord Death! Though we may think we have fooled Him for the time being, Lord Death always wins out in the end. Everyone else's version of life is only a make-believe story!

On the other hand, as someone else has said, history really means "His story," the Lord's story alone. Human beings are all really forms of God alone and ultimately all is nothing but the play of the Lord. Therefore, when we study *Itihāsa*, it is not for the usual purpose of merely learning dates, times, places, and events. We are not interested in these things in themselves, but through history we want to discover what the ultimate Truth is.

In Hinduism, the two famous books of *Itihāsa* are the *Rāmāyaṇa* and the *Mahābhārata*. They reveal the history of humanity as a whole and are not about one particular time-period alone. Therefore, if you read these two epics, you will know about World War

I, II, and every other war because it is actually the same story being repeated over and over again throughout history.

The Rāmāyaṇa

Though it is not possible here to relate in detail the story of the *Rāmāyaṇa*, I will touch on certain important points. The literal meaning of *Rāmāyaṇa* is "the life story of Rama." Rama was the Prince of Ayodhya, the son of King Dasharatha who was ruling the kingdom at that time. King Dasharatha had three wives to whom were born four sons. Sri Ramachandra was born to Queen Kausalya, Bharata to Queen Kaikeyi, and Lakshmana and Shatrughna to Queen Sumitra.

In its simplest form, the *Rāmāyaṇa* is the story of a great noble prince who was an ideal son, brother, disciple, husband, and king. Generally we find that a person is perfect in only one or maybe two relationships or fields of activity in life. One may be an ideal husband but not an ideal son; another may be an ideal son but a monstrous husband and an uncaring father. To find someone who is ideal in all of his or her relationships, in all fields of activity, and who is full of noble virtues is nearly impossible. Yet we find in the *Rāmāyaṇa,* Sri Ramachandra, who achieves what we consider "nearly impossible."

Sage Valmiki, who wrote the *Rāmāyaṇa*, presented Ramachandra as the perfect person because society is always in need of an ideal. It is a fact that when people have a higher goal in their lives, they strive hard to improve and bring out the best in themselves. But if one's ideal is low or if one has no higher goal to aspire to, one only drifts along in life and gets carried away by whatever whims and fancies are in his mind or in the society around him.

There are some people who believe that Sri Ramachandra was not an actual living person and that the *Rāmāyaṇa* is therefore imaginary, not historical. Why do we think in this way? Perhaps because we are rarely able to live up to even the simplest noble principle in our life, and we conclude, therefore, that as perfect a life as his is not possible. But such a view is false. Ramachandra was a living person, and, in fact, he lives even now in our hearts—

everywhere. The *Rāmāyaṇa* is not just a fictitious story or novel; it is true history. If it were merely a novel, it would never have gained such great respect, and even worship, that it now has.

Dharma Śāstra

Sri Ramachandra was not only an ideal man. It is said that he was a form of the Lord Himself, who came to earth and took human embodiment for our sake—to teach us how to live our lives correctly. Because Ramachandra's life was the embodiment of *dharma*, of righteousness, the *Rāmāyaṇa* is also considered to be a *dharma śāstra*. Its method of teaching is different from *śruti* and *smṛti*, however, in that the latter teach by way of commandments or injunctions—*prabhu vākya;* they state directly what one ought to do and what one ought not to do; what is right and what is wrong. But there is another way of teaching, called *mitra vākya*, by which we are given friendly advice as to what conduct is best to practice and what to avoid. As a *dharma śāstra*, the *Rāmāyaṇa* is considered to be *mitra vākya* (friendly advice).

Most of us, however, need more than just commandments or advice. We need demonstrations in practical life, and our question always is, "Has there ever been a person who has lived this life of perfection?" We want to see him, not off in the Himalayas somewhere, but right here in front of us, where we are now, going through all the ups and downs of life!

Sri Ramachandra was such a man of perfection. When you and I suffer in life, we usually complain and ask, "Why me?" But Sri Ramachandra, who was in the forest for fourteen years through no fault of his own, never complained. Even though we find him weeping at times for his father, for Sita, for Lakshmana, or for Bharata, if we look closely at his life, we see that what he loved most of all was *dharma*. For *dharma's* sake he was ready to give up everything, as he himself said in a famous *śloka*:

> As a king, the people are my deity, my altar of worship; and for their sake I will renounce whatever is demanded of me—my affection, compassion, happiness, or even Sita.

Even Maricha, the friend of Ravana, acknowledged Rama as the embodiment of *dharma*; and if one's own enemy gives such a certificate of approval, you know there must certainly be truth in it! If we cannot accept that such a person as Rama existed or if we think it is possible for him to live such a perfect life, but not ourselves, this is due to our own weakness of mind. In that case, the very purpose of the *Rāmāyaṇa* is defeated, for Rama came for the sole purpose to guide and help people like us to live as he did. This, in fact, is the specialty of the *Rāmāyaṇa*—that it demonstrates right conduct and shows how the higher values can be lived. In India, the *Rāmāyaṇa* is so popular that even those who are poorly educated know of it.

Once an old villager was reading the *Rāmāyaṇa* while sitting on a bench at the railway station waiting for the train to arrive. A young man with his wife was standing nearby and said to the old man, "You old-fashioned people read only that *Rāmāyaṇa* all the time. Do you not have any other book to read? There are so many best-sellers available these days. What is so great in the *Rāmāyaṇa* anyway?"

The old man continued to read and did not reply. The young man went away but came back after about half an hour, and when he saw the old man still reading, he became really annoyed and began to criticize the old man even more. Soon, however, the train arrived and everyone rushed in to get a seat, as one must do in India. It turned out that the old man and the young man were seated next to each other. The old man continued to read the *Rāmāyaṇa*. Suddenly the young man realized that his wife was missing! He looked for the emergency-chain to stop the train and shouted anxiously, "My wife! Where is she? I think she has been left behind on the platform!"

The old man said to him calmly, "If you had read *Rāmāyaṇa*, you would never have committed that mistake."

"What?" said the young man.

The old man explained: "It is said in the *Rāmāyaṇa* that when Ramachandra, Sita, and Lakshmana were standing on the bank of the *Gaṅgā* and the boatman came with his boat, Ramachandra asked

Sita to sit in the boat first and only then did he get in the boat himself! So why are you asking me what is said in the *Rāmāyaṇa* when you do not even know enough to take care of your wife and see that she gets into the train first? You see, the *Rāmāyaṇa* tells you even this!"

True enough, any time you are confused and cannot decide what your duty is, just read the *Rāmāyaṇa* and you will find the answer to all your doubts!

Solving Life's Conflicts

If we study the *Rāmāyaṇa* carefully, we will discover that not only are day-to-day duties demonstrated through Rama's example, but we are also taught how to deal with the greater conflicts in life, although the exact circumstances may be somewhat different. Consider, for example, how one day Sri Rama is told that he will be crowned king and the very next morning he is told that he must be exiled to the forest for fourteen years. The whole population of Ayodhya, as well as King Dasharatha, were begging him to stay, and though there were many other arguments against his going, Rama left for the forest, knowing it was his *dharma* to fulfill the boon his father had promised to Kaikeyi. This was a big decision to make—one which he made without showing any disappointment or bitterness.

On the other hand, Bharata's situation was more difficult. When he was told he had to become king in Rama's place, Bharata wondered at first whether he should do so. Rama himself tells Bharata that he should fulfill the wishes of their father and become king according to the second boon of Kaikeyi. But Bharata finally said, "No." How did he arrive at this conclusion? You see, in the law there is both the letter and the spirit. Which is more important? Naturally the spirit or intention is more important than the letter or literal meaning. Bharata knew that all the coronation arrangements had really been made for Ramachandra and that their father, King Dasharatha, had really decided to make Rama king, but had unfortunately been cornered by Kaikeyi. So Bharata asked himself, "Is it my *dharma* to fulfill my father's words or his wishes?" Realizing that his *dharma* was to fulfill his father's wishes, he did not accept the kingship.

These are the subtle ways by which we must determine our *dharma*. It is often difficult for people to determine *dharma* because, as it is said, "the mystery or the secret of *dharma* is hidden." The great importance of the *Rāmāyaṇa*, therefore, is that it teaches us how to observe situations and come to the right decision.

There is also a symbolic meaning in the story of the *Rāmāyaṇa*. I will just give the central ideas as there are many different interpretations.

A line from a beautiful song in the *Adhyātma Rāmāyaṇa* by Sadashiva Brahmendra tells the real identity of Sri Rama: "He who is sporting in my heart is Rama." Here Rama means "to sport, to revel." In another, it is said: "He who revels in the heart of all beings is Rama."

Another meaning of the name Rama is given in the *Rāmāyaṇa* itself: "Rama is that *sat-cit-ānanda* (existence-consciousness- bliss) *Brahman*, in which all yogis ever revel."

Rama is also, "He who delights everyone." What is that which delights everyone? If you ask a child, he may say, "Nintendo." Another person may say "Coke" or "money," but what actually delights everyone is joy, *ānanda*. It is not the toy, game, house, or money, but the joy that we derive from them. Therefore, Saint Tulsidas says:

> That ocean of bliss, a small droplet of which all the beings of all worlds take delight in, and depend upon for their happiness, that is Ramachandra.

The Symbolism of the Characters

Rama is *ānanda svarūpa*, the essence of joy, the *sat-cit-ānanda* playing in our heart. Therefore, the Rama about whom we read in the *Rāmāyaṇa* is actually our own absolute spiritual nature. And who is Sita to whom Rama is married? She is *śānti videhasutā sahacāriṇī*, the absolute peace wedded to our blissful nature (*ānanda svarūpa*). And the Ayodhya in which bliss and peace dwell together is the space in the heart.

In the story of the *Rāmāyaṇa*, Ramachandra had to cross the ocean to kill Ravana and Kumbhakarna. This ocean is the great ocean of ignorance and delusion that we must cross in order to destroy the enemies within us; the likes and dislikes, and the desire and anger. Only when these hosts of negative tendencies in our hearts are removed can we attain absolute peace.

Rama is also sometimes said to be *jñāna*, knowledge, and Sita, *bhakti*, devotion. Ravana, who is the embodiment of ignorance and delusion, ego and pride, can only be destroyed by Rama, who is pure Knowledge. Lakshmana is the incarnation of dispassion, Bharata the embodiment of love (of *Rāma prema*); and Shatrughna the embodiment of egoless service.

And what about Hanuman? Hanuman is very difficult to talk about because he is the embodiment of all the great divine qualities put together—devotion, dedication, service, dispassion, strength, humility, knowledge and every other virtue!

The other monkeys in Rama's army represent our numerous thoughts, some of which are not always directed toward the Lord alone. They also represent different kinds of spiritual disciplines, such as *japa*, austerity, or charity, in which we engage for other than purely spiritual purposes. This should not be the case, for all our spiritual endeavors should be dedicated to the Lord alone and not for any other reason, such as fame, wealth, or power. This is why it is said in a prayer: "Whatever I do, I dedicate to Lord Narayana." If you can do this you gain the real *Rāma rājya*, the kingdom of happiness, peace, and prosperity.

The *Rāmāyaṇa* is a poem, a story, an epic. But more than this, it is also a *dharma śāstra*, a demonstration of righteous living. Knowledge of almost every kind is found in the *Rāmāyaṇa*, including that taught in modern-day courses, such as economics, warfare, effective time management, and motivation theories. But of greatest importance is the fact that the *Rāmāyaṇa* is a manifestation of the Vedas and contains the highest spiritual knowledge (*Brahma vidyā* or *Ātma vidyā*). The epic is therefore also called *adhyātma śāstra*, a scripture that reveals the knowledge of the Self.

Thus, we can never really say that the *Rāmāyaṇa* is old. As we saw from the way people were glued to their television screens when the *Rāmāyaṇa* series was aired, the charm of *Rāmāyaṇa* can never fade away. It is ever fresh and new.

XVI

The Mahābhārata

Bhagavan Veda Vyasa was the first person to compile all the Vedas and teach them to his disciples, who, in turn, propagated these teachings among the populace. Vyasa found, however, that many people were unable to correctly discern the theme of the scriptures and he therefore asked his disciple, Jaimini Muni, to analyze the *karma* portion of the Vedas. This work became known as the *Karma Mīmāṃsā* or *Dharma Mīmāṃsā*, the exposition of *dharma*. Veda Vyasa himself composed the *Brahma Sūtras* to explain the subject matter of the Upanishads. Still Vyasa found that many people were incapable of understanding, at present or in the future, even the *Brahma Sūtras*, for they did not have enough patience, peace of mind, eagerness, or willingness to put forth the effort to study them. He therefore conceived the idea that this Knowledge should be brought out in a different form—as an *itihāsa*, history. The result was the *Mahābhārata*, which Veda Vyasa composed for people of all ages, all classes, educated or uneducated, in order to understand the theme of the Vedas.

Authorship

There are different opinions concerning the authorship of the *Mahābhārata*. One question raised is whether Veda Vyasa was one person or whether the name refers to more than one author. Another doubt raised is whether the entire 100,000 verses of the *Mahābhārata* were written in one time period or whether there were later additions by other writers. Some scholars contend that

Vyasa wrote only the first 40,000 verses and this book was named *Jaya*. Afterwards, other writers added more stories and it became known as *Bhārata*. Later, still more additions were made until the composition became the *Mahābhārata* as we know it today. As far as we are concerned, however, though these varying views exist, we believe that Veda Vyasa was one person and that he alone composed the entire *Mahābhārata*. Consisting of 100,000 verses, it is the world's largest epic in existence today, and an encyclopedia of knowledge.

A popular and very interesting story of how the *Mahābhārata* came to be written is contained in the epic itself—although most readers miss the main point of the story. It is said that when Veda Vyasa conceived the *Mahābhārata* in his mind he knew that it would be a very large work and that he would need a stenographer to take dictation. As Vyasa was thus contemplating, Lord Brahma appeared and told him to invoke Lord Ganesha, the god of knowledge, who would assist Vyasa in his work. Veda Vyasa invoked Lord Ganesha and when the latter appeared, Vyasa requested him to take dictation. Lord Ganesha said, "I am ready, but only on one condition: Once I start writing, you should not stop dictating to me." In other words, the dictation had to go on non-stop! We know how difficult this is nowadays, for when a boss dictates even one letter to his secretary, he has to stop again and again and say, "Wait! Read it back to me, please. What did I say so far?" Veda Vyasa thought this would be very difficult, but he did not want to lose the opportunity. So he said to Ganesha, "All right, I also have a condition: that you should not write down anything without grasping the full significance of what I say." This little point in the story highlights for us the seriousness, the depth, the preciousness, and the great value of the subject matter of the *Mahābhārata*.

As the story goes, Lord Ganesha and Vyasa agreed to each other's conditions and the dictation began. Now and then, however, Vyasa needed more time to think and compose more verses, so it is said that in those moments, he would dictate such a difficult verse that even Lord Ganesha had to stop to scratch his head and think deeply, "What is the meaning of this?" In that intervening period, Vyasa was able to compose his next verses.

We do not know even which verses Ganesha could not immediately understand, but it is said there may be at least 500 to 600 verses, the meaning of which are known only to Vyasa and Ganesha. A passage may appear as simple as a description of a river, a mountain, or a tree, but the verse may have a meaning far deeper than the superficial one. Therefore, the idea is that every verse must be thought over very deeply and carefully; none should be taken for granted. This is the significance of this simple story.

The *Mahābārata* contains every branch of knowledge, including science, arts, commerce, economics, politics, warfare, social science, history, mythology, *dharma śāstra*, and also *adhyātma śāstra*, the spiritual science of Self-knowledge. It is in the *Mahābhārata*, in fact, that we find the famous *Bhagavad Gītā*. If anyone asks what is in the *Mahābārata*, we answer, "What is not in it?" Veda Vyasa himself said: "What is in the *Mahābārata* is also in the world and what is not in the *Mahābārata* is not in the world." You may think this is a bold, egotistical statement, but it is not; and if you read this great epic carefully, you will understand that this claim is true.

It is also said that this entire world is what is left over by Veda Vyasa: *Vyāsocchiṣṭaṃ jagat sarvam. Ucchiṣṭaṃ* means left over—just as when we taste everything on our plates and leave the remaining portions. What is meant here is that Veda Vyasa has "tasted" or explained every branch of knowledge in the *Mahābārata*, and, consequently, whoever writes on any possible subject is really borrowing from the *Mahābārata*, either directly or indirectly!

The Central Theme

It is an interesting fact that in association with this great epic, the number eighteen constantly recurs: the 100,000 verses of the *Mahābārata* are divided into eighteen chapters or cantos called *parvans*; the Mahabharata War, which took place between the Kauravas and the Pandavas, lasted for eighteen days; the *Bhagavad Gītā*, placed in the middle of the *Mahābārata*, is divided into eighteen chapters; and also, the Puranas that Vyasa wrote are eighteen in number.

What is the significance of this number? According to Hindu tradition, the number eighteen stands for victory. This is why the *Mahābārata* was earlier called *Jaya*, which means victory. This number points out the very theme of the *Mahābārata*. Although essentially the main theme of the *Mahābārata* is the knowledge of the Vedas, in practical terms it represents victory over the lower self. The higher Self is the divinity that shines in our hearts; the lower self consists of our devilish tendencies and evil thoughts. To conquer these evil thoughts of the mind completely, once and for all, is the purpose for which the *Mahābārata* was written. This is the victory of Truth and *dharma*.

In the *Mahābārata* various characters repeatedly make the statement that the Pandavas will certainly win the war. Why is this so? Because, as it is said, "Where there is *dharma*, there is also victory." Bhagavan Sri Krishna told the Pandavas repeatedly that He was supporting them, not because they were His relatives or that He had any special love for them, but because they were following the path of *dharma*. Where *dharma* is, there the Lord is also; and where the Lord is, there must be victory. That is why it is said in the last verse of the *Gītā*:

> *Wherever Arjuna, the archer, is accompanied by Bhagavan Sri Krishna, the Lord of Yoga, there is victory and prosperity, divinity and nobility.* (XVIII:78)

Therefore, the lesson taught to us is this: If you want to have true, abiding victory, not just a temporary one, you must have the Lord on your side; and to have Him on your side, you must follow *dharma*. By conquering the mind of all the lower negative tendencies, we gain this real victory, wherein the enemy is defeated and complete and everlasting prosperity is achieved.

The depiction of the Mahabharata War in the outside world is also a reflection of the war within each one of us. There are people who say that the Mahabharata War did not actually take place—that it is only a symbolic story of the inner war. But if people are having a war in their own minds, do you think it will never be expressed outside? We see it happening every day. Even when a husband and wife have differences of opinion, do they not fight?

We cannot say that war is only on the inside, for whatever is inside us will also be expressed outside—in the family, the society, and the world.

Dharma Wins

This story of the Kauravas and Pandavas, of the struggle between good and evil, and the ultimate victory of the one who abides by *dharma* is pointed out. It is strange that we sometimes hear people say there is no use in being honest, righteous, or ethical. They say, "I tried being honest for a while but got no results. So I have given up the practice." But honesty is not a crash-course to be taken up for only fifteen days!

The scriptures say, "The lions in the forest kill and eat flesh. That is their *dharma* and no matter how hungry they are, they will not eat grass." You see, even the lions do not compromise their *dharma*! In the same way, the great saints, the *dharma sādhu puruṣas*, refuse to do other than what is *dharma*—even if it means great suffering or the threat of death. Similarly, only when we become uncompromising in our *dharma*, like the saints, will we win the real victory. This is the very quality which made the Pandavas great; and even though each of them had their own weaknesses, they would admit their faults and willingly suffer the consequences.

Although there are some people who say that good values, such as honesty and integrity, will not work in this present age of stress and strain, competition and politics, corruption and unequal distribution of wealth, is it really true that dishonesty wins and honesty loses? You may be surprised to know that even in dishonesty, honesty alone wins! Among gangsters and the Mafia, for instance, there is a lot of integrity and honesty. They are also very disciplined within their own groups, for if anyone waivers in his loyalty, they are removed from this world! So you see, even the evil forces gain their strength and victories due to these better values that operate within them. The evil succeed because of their unity. On the other hand, the so-called "good" people are not able to unite because each one wants to show off how wonderful he or she is. Therefore, they are really not such good people after all.

I read an article recently in which someone explained this fact very well. The writer said that if there is a fight between what is evil and truly good, good will win. Generally what we see are conflicts only between evil and lesser evil; yet we call that lesser evil "good." If I accuse another person by saying, "Oh, he swindled millions of dollars, but I only swindled one thousand dollars," this fact does not mean that I am a good person! I am just a person who is less bad!

Once I met a man who told me, "Swamiji, the whole society is corrupt! Everybody else is accepting bribes, but I have never accepted a bribe in my life."

I said, "Then you are really a wonderful person. How could you resist the temptation?"

He said, "Because no one offered it to me!"

When such a person remains incorrupt just because no one has tried to bribe or tempt him, we cannot really say that he is an honest person. When we see the so-called "good" losing against evil, it is only because the "good" are not truly good; they lack total integration and their goodness is mixed with other material values.

There are also those who are earning money by means fair or foul, who say that honesty does not work, yet expect their own treasurer or accountant to be very honest, and their friends or servants to be very loyal. So again, it is honesty and truthfulness that even the dishonest people respect. The irony is that the world always respects these great values most, but each of us wants to see them in other people, not in ourselves. We want everyone else to accept us as we are, but we will not accept others as they are. This is the problem.

Throughout the *Mahābārata* there are many secondary stories (*upākhyānas*), such as those of Nala and Damayanti, Dushyanta and Shakuntala, Yayati and Devayani. Each of these stories has its own purpose, but the main story around which the *Mahābārata* revolves is the conflict between the 100 evil-minded Kaurava brothers, including Duryodhana and Dushasana, and the noble Pandava brothers, who are only five in number: Yudhishthira, Bhima, Arjuna, Nakula, and Sahadeva. The Kauravas represent the forces of unrighteousness and negative tendencies, while the Pandavas represent the forces of righteousness and noble thoughts.

This conflict between good and evil has been going on in individual minds and in the world outside since time immemorial. It sometimes seems to us that evil wins more often than good. There are occasions when our divine and noble thoughts do conquer our temptations and corruptions, but then again, the good in us does not win a permanent victory; and we again give in to our lower tendencies. Why is this so? It is said that if the good forces fight the battle against evil on their own strength, these ups and downs, wins and losses, will always continue, but if the good take the support of the Lord, the victory of the good is permanent. This is why the Pandavas sought the help of Lord Krishna, who represents the higher spiritual Principle or Truth.

So what is the implication of this in our own personal lives? If I practice honesty, promptness, and good service only for the good name it will bring me, so that my business will run well and I will succeed financially, I am practicing these good values for the wrong reasons. When I practice noble virtues only for the sake of name, fame, or money, goodness lasts only until I discover that I can attain the same goals by dishonesty and hypocrisy. For the same reason, students are losing their faith in and their respect for the educational system—because today, education serves only to obtain a good job and to earn money, nothing more.

The practice of good qualities must always be directed toward and practiced for the sake of the Lord and spiritual enlightenment; then we will have the support of Truth and we will gain complete and permanent victory over the mind. Otherwise, the good in us will not last.

The Greatness of the Pandavas

In the *Mahābārata*, we find many different characters who are considered great and noble persons, yet who act at times in strange manners that we cannot justify. The *Mahābārata* presents the human struggle in its naked form, with all its strengths and weaknesses.

Veda Vyasa portrays human life as it is, without any make-up to hide the ugliness. This honest presentation is called *yathā vastu sthiti*, "as the fact is, so is it shown." There are many great men and women in this epic who also have their failings. When Vyasa brings out their greatness of character, he does not hide any of their weaknesses. But the fact that they have faults does not mean that their greatness is lost. It is whether or not they admit to their faults and try to overcome them and if they are ready to suffer the consequences that makes them great people.

In the *Bhāgavata Purāṇa* too, we find that Raja Parikshit commits a mistake in a fit of anger, when, being very hungry and thirsty one day after hunting, he puts a dead snake around the neck of a rishi who is in meditation. However, he does not thereafter start crying, "O God, please forgive me." No, he says, "I have done such a heinous crime, O Lord. Please give me a punishment such that I will never repeat this mistake." This was the greatness of King Parikshit. What we generally do, however, is to commit wrong actions and then say, "O Lord, please forgive me!"

We see that Yudhishthira, the eldest Pandava, had a weakness for gambling. The occasion for the notorious game with the Kauravas was not actually of his own choice, however, the rules at that time declared that if someone challenges you in a battle or a game, you cannot refuse the invitation. But when he did cross the limit due to his own weakness for gambling, Yudhishthira recognized his fault and told his brothers that they had to accept the consequences. For twelve years, he and his brothers had to live in exile in the forest and one year incognito, while all that time they were actually capable of attacking the Kauravas. Bhima and Arjuna used to become impatient and say, "Why not fight them now? We are completely capable!" But Yudhishthira said, "No, we have committed a mistake. We accepted their challenge and have lost it; therefore we must suffer. After our exile we will ask for what is rightfully ours, and if they do not give the kingdom to us, then we can engage in battle against them."

The Pandavas were great because they lived the nobler values of life, and whenever they did commit a mistake, they did not try to justify it, but were ready to suffer the consequences. The Lord does not reject a person just because he has a weakness; what he respects most is a person's honesty and integrity. Because Bhagavan Sri Krishna saw these qualities in the Pandavas, he told them, "I will support you fully." This is how the Pandavas were led to ultimate victory by the Lord.

XVII

The Characters of the Mahābhārata

In the *Mahābārata*, Veda Vyasa brings out human life in all its naked form and shows how men and women act and react to different experiences. He shows their greatness and their shallowness, meanness, and divinity, and an entire array of human emotions. Now we will look at a few characters of the *Mahābārata* and compare their emotions and attitudes with those in our own lives, for this *Itihāsa* is not the history of a past age alone—it is the history of humanity as a whole. Therefore, the lessons we learn from it are completely relevant even today.

Dhritarashtra

The name Dhritarashtra means he who holds a nation (*dhṛta*—holding on; *rāṣṭra*—nation). Though Dhritarashtra was the eldest of three brothers and had the right to the throne of Hastinapura, law prohibited him from becoming king because he was born blind. When his younger brother, Pandu, was made the next king, Dhritarashtra held a grudge against Pandu's family (the Pandavas) for the rest of his life. Later, when Pandu died suddenly in the forest, Dhritarashtra was given the responsibility of overseeing the kingdom until Pandu's eldest son, Yudhishthira, was old enough to become king. However, although Dhritarashtra knew that Yudhishthira should become king—not only according to law, but also because he was the best qualified of all the royal children,

Dhritarashtra was unable to give up his craving to become king. He tried, therefore, to fulfill his desire through his own eldest son, Duryodhana. Duryodhana was of a mean and wicked nature, yet Dhritarashtra was extremely attached to him.

We see again and again, the unsteadiness of Dhritarashtra's mind. On the one hand, he knows what is right and just; and even though he wants to do the right thing, his own ambition and attachment to his son makes him lose objectivity. Thus he becomes susceptible to the pressures put on him by Duryodhana and others to act improperly. Ultimately he yields to their wishes. We see this happen, for instance, when Dhritarashtra's youngest brother, Vidura, comes to advise him. Wise Vidura advises Dhritarashtra to give back to the Pandavas what is rightfully theirs and Dhritarashtra thinks, "Yes, that is the right thing to do and I should follow his advice." But then another wicked minister named Kanik, who is on Duryodhana's side, comes and gives him the opposite advice: "These Pandavas are your enemies and all enemies should be finished off completely." So Dhritarashtra changes his mind and starts thinking in the wrong direction again.

Is not our nature also like this? When we have ambitions that we cannot fulfill ourselves, we want to fulfill them through someone else. Then we become blind to justice. If we happen to be blessed with the company of wise and holy people, our minds start working in the right direction at that time and we think "Oh yes, how wonderful! This is the way I want to live." But as soon as we are in bad company again, our minds sink back into wrong channels of thinking and ultimately our strongest emotions take over.

Dhritarashtra was the only one who could have stopped the war, but because of his weakness, he did not. Instead he tried to shirk responsibility for his actions by evoking pity from others on account of his blindness. This is exactly what we do.

Reasons for Losing the War

In the Mahabharata War, though the Kaurava army was much larger than that of the Pandavas' and there were many great warriors on Duryodhana's side, such as Bhishma-Pitamaha, Dronacharya, and Kripacharya, the Kauravas were still defeated. Why did they lose the war? The main reason was that the Pandavas fought on the side of *dharma* and therefore had the help of the Lord, while the Kauravas fought on the side of *adharma* and thus did not have the Lord's help. Yet there were other reasons as well.

Another factor that caused the Kauravas' loss was that almost all the great leaders and armies who fought on their side really did so only for the sake of Bhishma and Dronacharya—not out of loyalty to Duryodhana or his cause. Yet Bhishma and Dronacharya themselves were divided in their hearts, for their love and blessings were with the Pandavas, and only their bodies were with the Kauravas. Now can a war ever be fought at all in this way? No matter how courageous and great the commanders of an army may be, if they do not have the conviction that what they are fighting for is right, there will be no strength behind their efforts.

Bhishma-Pitamaha, Dronacharya, and many other commanders and their warriors knew that the Kauravas stood for unrighteousness, and so their sympathies were really with the Pandavas. In fact, the Kaurava armies had in large measure been given to them by Lord Krishna Himself. When such a split between body and mind exists within the people, no one will be able to fight very well.

Attachment to Personal Vows

The question may arise in our mind as to why Bhishma and Dronacharya sided with the Kauravas even though they knew it was the side of *adharma*. In answering this, we see how helpless even great people become under the forces of their own wrong notions; and when they make a mistake, even the best have to pay for it.

Bhishma, the noble uncle of the Pandava and Kaurava children, is a great example of this. Many times, when the Kauravas were acting wrongfully, Bhishma simply watched them without saying a word. Consequently, although he himself was good and his whole life was one of self-sacrifice, he had to suffer by lying on a bed of arrows at the end of his life for all the times he had sided with *adharma*.

Why had he done this? In those days, people were very fond of taking vows. When Bhishma was still a boy, his father, the king, fell in love with a young girl and wanted to marry her. But the girl's father made a condition that the girl's own child must become king. For the sake of his father's happiness, Bhishma vowed never to become king and, secondly, never to marry or have children (who would be possible threats to the throne). Bhishma's vows shows how self-sacrificing he was. Yet the mistake he made was to further vow that he would always be loyal to whoever sat on the throne of Hastinapura. This led to a serious problem later when Dhritarashtra was ruling. Bhishma sometimes wept for the sad state of affairs in Hastinapura, but he was obliged to remain loyal to Dhritarashtra. Bhishma took the position of a servant, which in itself is good. But what is the use of such loyalty to an unrighteous king who is bringing about the downfall of the whole nation?

The point is that we should know when to follow a vow according to word and when to fulfill it according to spirit. Though Bhishma was great, he gave undue importance to abiding by the spoken word rather than fulfilling *dharma* in a larger sense, for the good of all.

This excessive fondness for taking individual pledges or vows (*pratijñās*) and the refusal to break them was another problem which led to the Kauravas' downfall. For when an individual is more concerned with himself than with the welfare of the whole, the very purpose for which the vow was made is defeated. In short, the reasons for the Kauravas' downfall were: 1) the commanders and warriors did not have complete loyalty to the cause; 2) even the loyalty to the side of *adharma* was due to their wrong notions concerning individual honor.

Advice of Lord Krishna

The Pandavas and other leaders on their side also had this habit of taking vows, which later got them into trouble. Fortunately, however, they always had Lord Krishna with them to interpret the vows in the proper way. For example, Arjuna once vowed that he would kill anyone who insulted him, his valor, or his Gandiva bow. It so happened that one day, on the battlefield, Yudhishthira was angry at Arjuna and cursed in frustration, "Fie on your Gandiva bow!" Arjuna cried, "What did you say?" and immediately pulled out his bow to kill Yudhishthira.

It would have been terrible if Arjuna had killed his older brother; therefore, Lord Krishna told him, "Arjuna, do not be foolish. Certainly you should fulfill this vow if you have taken it, but it is also said that one's father or brother can be killed by means other than physical destruction. If one dishonors, insults, or abuses them verbally, it is as good as killing them. So you can kill Yudhishthira, but only with words, not arrows." Arjuna then scolded Yudhishthira severely. Afterwards, Sri Krishna told Arjuna to do *namaskāra* (prostration) to his brother for having spoken to him in such a manner.

Luckily, the Pandavas listened to the Lord when He advised them, for the war was not for the glory of an individual. If they had held onto their own petty little vows, their very reason for fighting the war would have been in vain.

Lord Krishna Himself was an example of how a vow should be fulfilled in a way beneficial to all. He had told Arjuna earlier, "I will advise you during the war, but I will not take up a weapon in my hand." When Bhishma heard about Sri Krishna's vow, he said to himself, "I am going to make him take up a weapon!" Bhishma fought such a terrible battle with Arjuna that if Sri Krishna had not stepped in, Arjuna and the whole Pandava army would have been destroyed. Realizing this threat, Sri Krishna took up a chariot wheel in his hands and rushed toward Bhishma. Arjuna cried, "Bhagavan, stop! You vowed you would not take up a weapon!" But Krishna told him to forget about it. Bhishma dropped his weapons and said, "O Lord, please kill me, for such a death would be a very great blessing." When Sri Krishna saw that Bhishma had thrown down his weapons, He cooled down and did not strike Bhishma.

Therefore, the important question to consider always is: Do I regard my own individual honor and glory as greater than the cause of *dharma* and the total nation's glory, or is *dharma* greater than me?

Dronacharya

Dronacharya was also a great person, but he too was not free from faults. Since he was born as a brahmin, there was no need, nor was it his duty, to learn archery and warfare. Yet, due to such a desire as a young boy, Dronacharya went to a *gurukula* to be instructed in these arts. There he became friends with Drupada, who was the crown prince of a nearby kingdom. Drupada promised that when he would become king, Dronacharya could come to him for anything he might need. Years later, however, when Dronacharya went to him to ask for one cow because of his poverty, Drupada became arrogant and pretended not to know him. Dronacharya felt terribly humiliated and angry, and vowed to take revenge.

Incapable of fulfilling his ambition for revenge himself, Drona wanted to fulfill his desire through someone else. He went to Hastinapura and there became the archery instructor for the Kaurava and Pandava boys. When their training was over and it came time for the boys to give *gurudakṣiṇā* (gift to the teacher), Drona thought to himself, "Ah, now is my chance!" and told them to capture Drupada and bring him there. Drupada was captured and dragged into Dronacharya's presence, and Drona forgave him. However, Drupada then felt so insulted and enraged that he swore to have a son who would kill Dronacharya. Thus the cycle continued!

We can see then that even while Dronacharya was serving in the Kaurava palace, he was doing so only with his own personal ambition in mind. Also, his reactions of anger and vengeance were just the opposite of true brahmin qualities. Furthermore, he degraded himself by becoming a paid, hired tutor for the royal children. This is why we are warned in the *Mahābārata* that "man is the slave of money, but money is not the slave of anyone."

When some people read the *Mahābārata*, they wonder why all

these questionable characters are portrayed, since the *Mahābārata* is said to be a representation of the great Hindu culture. But it is not meant that each character is ideal or that we should glorify and follow the example of those with such negative qualities. We are simply being shown, through the characters, all possible patterns of human behavior, responses, thoughts, and attitudes—so that we can learn from these examples what is right and wrong, which kind of behavior leads to happiness, and which does not. The cause for the Kauravas' defeat lay in the fact that even though the great leaders knew in their conscience what was right, they could not rise above their own individual weaknesses, attachments, and ambitions.

I repeat, however, that even with these drawbacks, their greatness was not completely lost, for many of them were great in other roles or activities. When Dronacharya, for instance, heard that his son, Ashvatthaman, had died in battle, Dronacharya sat down in meditation and gave up his body at will. This shows the power of the spiritual practice he had done in the past, and this much greatness on his part we must accept. Unfortunately, during his lifetime this greatness was blemished by his other weaknesses.

Kunti

Queen Kunti, the mother of the Pandavas, was one of the greatest devotees of the Lord. All her children were born of celestial deities as the result of a mantra she chanted to invoke them. However, because her eldest son, Karna, was born to her before her marriage, she hid him away, after which, he was found and raised by a *śūdra* family. Although she was a great person, Kunti's one fault was that she could never gather the courage until the last minute to admit that Karna was her own son. As a result, a deep rivalry developed between Karna and Arjuna, even from their youth, because Dronacharya loved Arjuna very much, but he refused to teach Karna, since the boy was not considered to be of royal parentage. This feeling of competition in Karna gave rise to the same feeling in Arjuna.

All this happened because Kunti could not admit she was Karna's mother. Of course, we can understand the other social pressures she was under to conceal this fact; but one must weigh the consequences of hiding the truth against one's own personal benefit. History could have been different if she had told the truth. Just before the war started, Kunti finally revealed to Karna the truth of his birth, which made him feel torn. Thereafter, he was unable to fight the battle wholeheartedly.

Duryodhana and Dushasana

Just as there was brotherly love between the Pandava brothers, there was also brotherly love between Duryodhana and Dushasana. Dushasana, however, was just a shadow of Duryodhana and would follow him in whatever wicked plan the elder brother had. Yes, Dushasana rose above his individuality in a sense, but only for the sake of his wicked brother. This shows us that loyalty is good and meaningful only when it is for a noble cause; otherwise, it is useless and creates problems.

Thus we find on this large canvas of the *Mahābārata* the innumerable intrigues and conspiracies of the royal palace, how and when the human personality reacts when insulted or dishonored, and how long the mind dwells upon it and seeks the destruction of the offender.

Shakuni

Shakuni, who later became the notorious cheat at dice, felt very insulted when the forefathers of the later Kaurava brothers (the Kuru vamshins), approached his father, Gandhara Naresha, and asked to have Shakuni's sister, Gandhari, as Dhritarashtra's wife. Shakuni thought, "How can my good sister be given to a blind man?" Because the Kurus were physically and politically powerful, Shakuni let them take her, but in his mind he vowed to see to it that they would all be destroyed.

As we can see, each character in the Kaurava camp was bent upon destroying someone—each playing his own game, for his own purpose. In effect, the Kauravas were all split within themselves and amongst themselves.

Yudhishthira

Yudhishthira, as noted before, was a very good person, but he had a weakness for playing dice. Consequently, he was later trapped by Shakuni and others in the dice game. See how even one small weakness ends up in disaster when one crosses the limit!

Another lesson of the *Mahābārata* is that the policy of appeasement does not work. Though Yudhishthira should have become the crowned prince of Hastinapura, Duryodhana wanted the whole kingdom for himself. For the sake of avoiding war, for Bhishma and others, and because Veda Vyasa had warned Yudhishthira to beware of the Kauravas, Yudhishthira agreed to split the kingdom with Duryodhana! But by splitting the kingdom, do you think the problem could be solved? No, especially not when Duryodhana was greedy for the whole country. There is a common saying: "If you feed milk to a snake, the snake remains poisonous." He does not, thereby, become a milky snake! The milk will only turn to poison. Therefore, even Yudhishthira's forgiving of the Kauravas and yielding to their demands went past the limit.

Bhishma

Bhishma-Pitamaha had his weaknesses, but he did not justify his faults. At the end of his life, he knew that each arrow in his bed of arrows represented an occasion when he had followed *adharma*. Swami Chinmayananda says, in fact, that Bhishma is the real hero of the *Mahābārata* story, for the whole epic begins and ends with him. Though he served Dhritarashtra, he never did anything for his own enjoyment. He was a devotee of Lord Krishna, and in the *Śrīmad Bhāgavata*, it is said that as Bhishma lay on the bed of arrows, Lord Krishna said to all present, "Here is a great soul. From him you can learn *dharma* in its entirety." Bhishma had waited to die until Lord Krishna came to him, and when the Lord arrived, the Lord said to Bhishma, "Not only should you chant my Name, but also fix your mind on Me, see Me with your eyes, and merge in Me." Then, while Yudhishthira questioned Bhishma on *dharma*, the Lord relieved the dying man of all pain so that

Bhishma could answer and teach everyone the knowledge of *dharma*. At this time, many great people honored Bhishma; Lord Krishna bestowed His grace on him; and even the gods showered flowers.

The Cause of Righteousness

Read the *Mahābārata* and think about it. In our own personalities and lives we see these same contradictions, the same problems and struggles. We see certain characters in the *Mahābārata*, like Yudhishtira, whose motives were good. But having good motives alone is not enough. Some characters had strong personalities, and though essentially good, they fell short of the greater ideal. Some, on the other hand, were positively wicked, like Duryodhana. Interestingly, it was Veda Vyasa, whose children and grandchildren the Kauravas and Pandavas really were, who remained ever aloof from the whole situation and wrote down this history of all his children.

The Pandavas won the war because they were on the side of *dharma* and had the help of Lord Krishna. Whenever there was a question concerning *dharma*, the Lord was there to interpret it properly, and the Pandavas readily followed His advice. On the Pandava side there was no splitting of hearts, for all had total loyalty and full conviction in their cause. This is how they were led to victory by the Lord.

In short, when the society is good but the individual puts himself above *dharma*, the individual brings himself to destruction. If society as a whole is bad, the individual who stands up for *dharma* becomes great. Therefore, the cause of righteousness is of greatest value and should be put above everything else. This is the great lesson of the *Mahābārata*.

XVIII

The Purāṇas

Our last topic concerns the class of literature called *Purāṇas*, otherwise known as mythology. This literature is much misunderstood by those who have read either little or nothing of it. Some people say that the *Purāṇas* are nothing but fictional stories. When we read them, the question of whether the stories are factual or imaginary always arises.

Let us begin by saying that they are not imaginary. Earlier, when we were discussing the *Itihāsa*, the *Rāmāyaṇa* and the *Mahābārata*, we observed that to understand the theme of the Vedas completely, we must study and understand the *Itihāsa* and the *Purāṇas*. This is because their theme and purpose is one—to reveal the *Paramātman*, the absolute Reality. The literal meaning of *purāṇa* is ancient, and the *Ātman*, the Self, is Itself called *Purāṇa*, the most ancient One. Yet it is not ancient in the general sense of old. Our idea of old and new is always within the framework of time, but when we refer to the Self as being ancient, it is not with reference to time. It is That from which even the concept of time arose. Therefore, this "ancient One," the supreme Self, is timeless.

Sri Shankaracharya explains the word *purāṇa* as: that which, even though it is old, is ever new. How can a thing be old and new at the same time? This is possible only for something that is unconditioned by time. A timeless factor does not age; it is ever fresh, ever new. The implied meaning of *purāṇa* is, therefore, that which is ever new.

Spiritual Lessons

This absolute Reality revealed by the *Purāṇas* is also the theme of the Vedas and Upanishads, but the method of revelation is unique in the *Purāṇas*. They tell many stories, some of which are historical and others metaphorical, but they are full of lessons. The *Purāṇas* themselves point out which stories are symbolic.

There is a difference between *Itihāsa* (history) and *Purāṇas* (mythology), which we should clarify. The *Itihāsa* is said to be *ghaṭana pradhāna*, literature which is fact-oriented, because it is an account of historical facts and events as they took place. On the other hand, the *Purāṇas* are *śikṣā pradhāna*, education-oriented, in which stories are told in order to teach lessons. In a history book, one cannot include an imaginary story, but in the *Purāṇas*, this is done for a purpose. Yet as we read them, we should not constantly be wondering whether the event did or did not take place. It may or may not have. In the stories of the tiger, lion, monkey, or fox, one need not ask, "How can a monkey speak?" This is not the point. The question is, "What do we learn from the story?"

The Five Topics

The *Purāṇas* reveal the Truth through the discussion of five major topics.

1) *Sarga*: creation of the fundamental elements
2) *Pratisarga*: creation of variety
3) *Manvantara*: the terms of the Manus
4) *Vaṃśa*: the lunar and solar dynasties
5) *Vaṃśānucarita*: the lives of individuals born in these dynasties.

Sarga is the creation of the elements, the fundamental particles, or raw materials, from which all other things are made. From these five elements the entire variety of individual beings and things is created. This secondary creation is called *pratisarga* or *visarga*. To give an example, a potter cannot make his variety of clay pots unless the clay already exists. Thus the primary creation, the clay, would be called *sarga* and the secondary creation, the various individual pots, would be called *pratisarga*.

The entire world is full of plurality, the variety of objects and beings, each of which is distinct from the other. We see this clearly, but from where has this plurality come? If we look at the material causes of all of them, they are the same: space, air, fire, water, and earth. All of us have in common a physical body, sense organs, mind, and intellect. But look how diverse they are! It is said that this creation of multiplicity is according to *tattva* and *karma*, each individual's nature and action.

Through this discussion of *sarga* and *visarga,* we are shown first the plurality of creation; then this plurality is reduced to its common factors—the five elements. We are led further to inquire into the origin of these common factors, and finally it is said that all this has come out of the *Paramātman*, the *Purāṇa*. In this way, the highest Truth is indicated.

Manvantara

The third topic of the *Purāṇas* is *Manvantara*. When we look at humanity as a whole, we find the tendency to disobey the laws of nature—and every other law! Other creatures instinctively abide by nature's law, but a human being must be told what to do. He must know his *dharma* and how to live it. Just as there is a president or chairman in charge of the department of religion in the government or the universities, Manu is in charge of the universal department of religion and *dharma*. Each cycle, during which one Manu rules over this creation, is called a *manvantara*.

In the Hindu tradition, time is divided into four *yugas,* or ages: *satya yuga*, *tretā yuga*, *dvāpara yuga*, and *kali yuga*. All four put together are equivalent to one *mahā yuga*, which is calculated to be about four million years. One thousand *mahā yugas* constitute one day of Brahmaji, the Creator. In this one day, fourteen Manus fulfill their terms. And when a new Manu comes to rule, the whole heavenly cabinet—the presiding gods of the cosmic order—changes. Therefore, the term of each Indra, Varuna, and Agni is only for one *manvantara*.

The Manu who is in charge during a particular time must see to it that *dharma* is followed by all in the world, and sometimes he must provide new interpretations of *dharma*, as required. How does he do this? By sending saints, sages, devotees, and other religious interpreters into the world to teach the rest of us the right way to live. Even today, when there is so much *adharma* in the world and people are very extroverted, there are still many individuals pursuing this spiritual knowledge. It is Manu who makes this possible.

When we think of this vast flow of time indicated in the *Purāṇas*, our intellects become stunned. We cannot conceive of the beginning, middle, or end of time, space, and this creation of beings. Finally the scriptures say that all this exists in one tiny particle of *Brahman*. To think of creation itself is mind-boggling. To contemplate on the infinitude of the Lord forces our vision to expand even more!

Thus, through *sarga* (fundamental creation) and *pratisarga* (particular creation), the *Paramātman* is indicated. And in the *manvantara* we are shown that by following *dharma* our minds will be purified and we will realize the Self.

The Solar and Lunar Dynasties

The fourth topic in the *Purāṇas* is *vaṃśa*, meaning dynasties. We are told that there were two dynasties ruling the world: the *Sūrya Vaṃśa*, or solar dynasty, and the *Candra Vaṃśa*, or lunar dynasty. The biographies of the kings, sages, rishis, and common people born into these dynasties are described in the *vaṃśānucarita*. Many were great souls; many were not. Some were wicked and some were ordinary people.

What is the reason for describing these two dynasties? From the good people we learn how we *should* live our lives and from the wicked, who destroyed themselves, we learn how *not* to live our lives. Some who were wicked in the beginning and spent their time indulging in sense pleasures achieved greatness later through their associations with holy people. Therefore, we should not become depressed about ourselves, for if some of these wicked or sensuous people became great, why can we not become great as well?

Means of Knowledge

Another important question is: What status do the *Purāṇas* hold as a means of knowledge? Human life is meant for gaining knowledge, and in order to gain knowledge, we must have a means of knowledge. There are many means of knowledge (*pramāṇas*), but only three main ones: direct perception (*pratyakṣa*), inference (*anumāna*), and oral testimony (*śabda*). We gather the knowledge of sound, color, form, taste, touch, and smell through direct perception. Inference is knowledge of the existence of a thing through the perception of something else. For instance, when we see smoke we know there must be fire somewhere. Or, if I see a certain car outside a house, I may infer the presence of a friend inside.

Śabda, however, gives us knowledge or information of an existing fact through the spoken or written word. For instance, if you receive a telegram that a family member is sick, you have neither inferred that fact nor seen it, but you have received the information through words. Most of our knowledge, in fact, is gained through *śabda*, for how much have we come to know through actual seeing? Very little indeed. Our knowledge of history, geography, and current events, for example, is almost entirely through *śabda pramāṇa*.

Both the Vedas and the *Purāṇas* are regarded as *śabda pramāṇa*, yet the specialty of the *Purāṇas* is that they are also *sambhava pramāṇa*, a means to know (*pramāṇa*) the possibilities of things not yet seen (*sambhava*). We can know facts as they exist (*tattva*), and from them, imagine the possibility of other things.

Thus we read certain stories in the *Purāṇas* and wonder whether such a thing can happen. For example, there is one story of a man who went to take a bath in a lake, and when he came out, he was a woman. There is another story of a king who was a man for six months of the year and a woman for the other six months. His subjects got fed up with the situation, as you can imagine! The point is that anything is possible. Even today there is an operation for a sex change, and if not physically transformed, a man may at least behave like a woman and wear the clothes of a woman.

that were considered fiction years ago have become reality today. Even the mind's wildest imaginations have the possibility of becoming actualized. Perhaps they even already exist somewhere. Many times thoughts come into our minds, which at first we take to be impossibilities, but later discover their existence through books or other means. Then we realize that there is nothing that is impossible. Even science fiction books give rise to new ideas that set other scientists thinking and making discoveries.

Thus the job of *pramāṇa* is not only to reveal a thing as it is, but also to present the possibilities of many other things. We think certain things are impossible because we believe whatever little we know is alone what the world is. But do we know how expansive the universe is, how many cosmoses there are, or how many beings exist on different stars and planets? We see such a tiny, limited part of the world, and yet we make assumptions as if we knew this entire creation.

But the many worlds and beings we read about in the *Purāṇas* are described only to point out to us the one Reality, the origin of all this creation, the very substratum and sustaining factor of the world, to which the whole world returns. That is *Brahman*, the *Paramātman*.

The One Reality

There are eighteen *Purāṇas* in all, including the *Brāhma Purāṇa*, *Śiva Purāṇa*, *Viṣṇu Purāṇa*, *Gaṇeśa Purāṇa*, *Garuḍa Purāṇa*, and others. In the *Viṣṇu Purāṇa* it is said that the absolute Reality is Vishnu and that this entire creation, the forces of nature, their presiding deities, and all other gods came out of Lord Vishnu. In the *Śiva Purāṇa* it is said that Shiva is the absolute Reality and that creation came out of Him. The same thing is said in the *Gaṇeśa Purāṇa*, and all the others. When people read these apparently conflicting stories, they become very confused. But there is confusion only if we do not have proper understanding and if we think that the names Vishnu, Shiva, or Ganesha refer only to the Lord in that particular form.

The Truth pointed out in all the *Purāṇas* is that there is only

The Truth pointed out in all the *Purāṇas* is that there is only one absolute Reality, *Brahman*, from which everything has emerged. In the *Gaṇeśa Purāṇa* that Reality will be indicated by the word "Ganesha"; while in the *Śiva Purāṇa* the name "Shiva" will be used to refer to that Reality. Although all deities have a second "identity," in charge of particular cosmic functions, and are also known in their various incarnations on earth (that is, Vishnu as Rama and Krishna), their absolute identity is the same. As it is said, "Truth is One, sages call It by many names." When we realize this, we will not become confused.

Along these same lines, an interesting story is told in the *Śiva Purāṇa* about Lord Shiva's marriage. As was the custom then, Shiva, the groom, was asked, "What is your lineage? Who is your father?" Shiva replied, "My father is Lord Brahma." "Who is your grandfather?" they asked Him. Shiva said, "Vishnu is my grandfather." Finally they asked Him, "Who is the father of Vishnu?" and Shiva replied, "I am the father of Vishnu!"

Lord Shiva was trying to say that as an individual entity, he would have to answer that "so and so" was his father or grandfather; but if asked further, from the highest standpoint, He would have to admit, "I am the cause of this entire creation!"

In conclusion, *purāṇa* means ancient, in the sense of timeless, eternal. The *Purāṇic* literature reveals this absolute Reality by a unique method of story-telling, which is *śikṣā pramāṇa*, education-oriented. The *Purāṇas* are also *sambhava pramāṇa*, a means by which we come to know things not only as they are, but also the possibility of things which could exist in another place and time. This *Paramātman*, the highest Reality, is revealed through the five topics of *sarga*, *pratisarga*, *manvantara*, *vaṃśa*, and *vaṃśānucarita*. The same Reality is indicated by all eighteen *Purāṇas*, though by different names, such as Shiva, Vishnu, Ganesha, and so on. This, in brief, is the essence of *Purāṇic* literature.

Pronunciation of Sanskrit Letters

a	(b*u*t)
ā	(mom)
i	(*i*t)
ī	(b*ee*t)
u	(s*u*ture)
ū	(p*oo*l)
ṛ	(r*i*g)
ṝ	(*rrri*g)
ḷ	no English equivalent
e	(pl*a*y)
ai	(h*i*gh)
o	(t*oe*)
au	(c*ow*)
k	(s*k*ate)
kh	(*K*ate)
g	(*g*ate)
gh	(*g*awk)
ṅ	(si*ng*)
c	(*ch*unk)
ch	(mat*ch*)
jh	(*J*ohn)
jh	(*j*am)
ñ	(bu*n*ch)
ṭ, ṭh	no English equivalent
ḍ, ḍh, ṇ	no English equivalent
t	(*t*ell)
th	(*t*ime)
d	(*d*uck)
dh	(*d*umb)
n	(*n*umb)
p	(s*p*in)
ph	(*p*in)
b	(*b*un)
bh	(ru*b*)
m	(*m*uch)
y	(*y*oung)
r	(d*r*ama)
l	(*l*uck)
v	(*w*ile/*v*ile)
s	(*sh*ove)
ṣ	(bu*sh*el)
s	(*s*o)
h	(*h*um)
ṁ	(nasalization of preceding vowel)
ḥ	(aspiration of preceding vowel)